THE WANDERING JEW

BOOK I

Eugene Sue

1st WORLD
LIBRARY
Literary Society

The Wandering Jew, Book I

Eugene Sue

© 1st World Library, 2006
PO Box 2211
Fairfield, IA 52556
www.1stworldlibrary.com
First Edition

LCCN: 2006935217

Softcover ISBN: 1-4218-2470-1
Hardcover ISBN: 1-4218-2370-5
eBook ISBN: 1-4218-2570-8

Purchase *"The Wandering Jew, Book I"*
as a traditional bound book at:
www.1stWorldLibrary.com/purchase.asp?ISBN=1-4218-2470-1

1st World Library is a literary, educational organization dedicated to:

- Creating a free internet library of downloadable ebooks

- Hosting writing competitions and offering book publishing scholarships.

Interested in more 1st World Library books?
contact: literacy@1stworldlibrary.com
Check us out at: www.1stworldlibrary.com

1st World Library Literary Society

Giving Back to the World

"If you want to work on the core problem, it's early school literacy."

- James Barksdale, former CEO of Netscape

"No skill is more crucial to the future of a child, or to a democratic and prosperous society, than literacy."

- Los Angeles Times

Literacy... means far more than learning how to read and write... The aim is to transmit... knowledge and promote social participation."

- UNESCO

"Literacy is not a luxury, it is a right and a responsibility. If our world is to meet the challenges of the twenty-first century we must harness the energy and creativity of all our citizens."

- President Bill Clinton

"Parents should be encouraged to read to their children, and teachers should be equipped with all available techniques for teaching literacy, so the varying needs and capacities of individual kids can be taken into account."

- Hugh Mackay

A NOTE ON THE AUTHOR OF THE
WANDERING JEW - EUGENE SUE (1804-1857)

Time and again physicians and seamen have made noteworthy reputations as novelists. But it is rare in the annals of literature that a man trained in both professions should have gained his greatest fame as a writer of novels. Eugene Sue began his career as a physician and surgeon, and then spent six years in the French Navy. In 1830, when he returned to France, he inherited his father's rich estate and was free to follow his inclination to write. His first novel, "Plick et Plock", met with an unexpected success, and he at once foreswore the arts of healing and navigation for the precarious life of a man of letters. With varying success he produced books from his inexhaustible store of personal experiences as a doctor and sailor. In 1837, he wrote an authoritative work on the French Navy, "Histoire de la marine Francaise".

More and more the novel appealed to his imagination and suited his gifts. His themes ranged from the fabulous to the strictly historical, and he became popular as a writer of romance and fictionized fact. His plays, however, were persistent failures. When he published "The Mysteries of Paris", his national fame was assured, and with the writing of "The Wandering Jew" he achieved world-wide renown. Then, at the height of his literary career, Eugene Sue was driven into exile after Louis Napoleon overthrew the Constitutional Government in a coup d'etat and had himself officially proclaimed Emperor Napoleon III. The author of "The Wandering Jew" died in banishment five years later.

CONTENTS

PROLOGUE

THE LAND'S END OF TWO WORLDS

The Arctic Ocean encircles with a belt of eternal ice the desert confines of Siberia and North America - the uttermost limits of the Old and New worlds, separated by the narrow, channel, known as Behring's Straits.

The last days of September have arrived.

The equinox has brought with it darkness and Northern storms, and night will quickly close the short and dismal polar day. The sky of a dull and leaden blue is faintly lighted by a sun without warmth, whose white disk, scarcely seen above the horizon, pales before the dazzling, brilliancy of the snow that covers, as far as the eyes can reach, the boundless steppes.

To the North, this desert is bounded by a ragged coast, bristling with huge black rocks.

At the base of this Titanic mass lied enchained the petrified ocean, whose spell-bound waves appear fired as vast ranges of ice mountains, their blue peaks fading away in the far-off frost smoke, or snow vapor.

Between the twin-peaks of Cape East, the termination of Siberia, the sullen sea is seen to drive tall icebergs across a streak of dead green. There lies Behring's Straits.

Opposite, and towering over the channel, rise the granite masses of Cape Prince of Wales, the headland of North America.

These lonely latitudes do not belong to the habitable world; for the piercing cold shivers the stones, splits the trees, and causes the earth to burst asunder, which, throwing forth showers of icy spangles seems capable of enduring this solitude of frost and tempest, of famine and death.

And yet, strange to say, footprints may be traced on the snow, covering these headlands on either side of Behring's Straits.

On the American shore, the footprints are small and light, thus betraying the passage of a woman.

She has been hastening up the rocky peak, whence the drifts of Siberia are visible.

On the latter ground, footprints larger and deeper betoken the passing of a man. He also was on his way to the Straits.

It would seem that this man and woman had arrived here from opposite directions, in hope of catching a glimpse of one another, across the arm of the sea dividing the two worlds - the Old and the New.

More strange still! the man and the woman have crossed the solitudes during a terrific storm! Black pines, the growth of centuries, pointing their bent heads in different parts of the solitude like crosses in a churchyard, have been uprooted, rent, and hurled aside by the blasts!

Yet the two travellers face this furious tempest, which has plucked up trees, and pounded the frozen masses into splinters, with the roar of thunder.

They face it, without for one single instant deviating from the straight line hitherto followed by them.

Eugene Sue

Who then are these two beings who advance thus calmly amidst the storms and convulsions of nature?

Is it by chance, or design, or destiny, that the seven nails in the sole of the man's shoe form a cross - thus:

$$*$$
$$*\ *\ *$$
$$*$$
$$*$$
$$*$$

Everywhere he leaves this impress behind him.

On the smooth and polished snow, these footmarks seem imprinted by a foot of brass on a marble floor.

Night without twilight has soon succeeded day - a night of foreboding gloom.

The brilliant reflection of the snow renders the white steppes still visible beneath the azure darkness of the sky; and the pale stars glimmer on the obscure and frozen dome.

Solemn silence reigns.

But, towards the Straits, a faint light appears.

At first, a gentle, bluish light, such as precedes moonrise; it increases in brightness, and assumes a ruddy hue.

Darkness thickens in every other direction; the white wilds of the desert are now scarcely visible under the black vault of the firmament.

Strange and confused noises are heard amidst this obscurity.

They sound like the flight of large night - birds - now flapping now-heavily skimming over the steppes-now descending.

But no cry is heard.

This silent terror heralds the approach of one of those imposing phenomena that awe alike the most ferocious and the most harmless, of animated beings. An Aurora Borealis (magnificent sight!) common in the polar regions, suddenly beams forth.

A half circle of dazzling whiteness becomes visible in the horizon. Immense columns of light stream forth from this dazzling centre, rising to a great height, illuminating earth, sea, and sky. Then a brilliant reflection, like the blaze of a conflagration, steals over the snow of the desert, purples the summits of the mountains of ice, and imparts a dark red hue to the black rocks of both continents.

After attaining this magnificent brilliancy, the Northern Lights fade away gradually, and their vivid glow is lost in a luminous fog.

Just then, by a wondrous mirage an effect very common in high latitudes, the American Coast, though separated from Siberia by a broad arm of the sea, loomed so close that a bridge might seemingly be thrown from one world to other.

Then human forms appeared in the transparent azure haze overspreading both forelands.

On the Siberian Cape, a man on his knees, stretched his arms towards America, with an expression of inconceivable despair.

On the American promontory, a young and handsome woman replied to the man's despairing gesture by pointing to heaven.

For some seconds, these two tall figures stood out, pale and shadowy, in the farewell gleams of the Aurora.

But the fog thickens, and all is lost in the darkness.

Eugene Sue

Whence came the two beings, who met thus amidst polar glaciers, at the extremities of the Old and New worlds?

Who were the two creatures, brought near for a moment by a deceitful mirage, but who seemed eternally separated?

CHAPTER I

MOROK

The month of October, 1831, draws to its close.

Though it is still day, a brass lamp, with four burners, illumines the cracked walls of a large loft, whose solitary window is closed against outer light. A ladder, with its top rungs coming up through an open trap leads to it.

Here and there at random on the floor lie iron chains, spiked collars, saw-toothed snaffles, muzzles bristling with nails, and long iron rods set in wooden handles. In one corner stands a portable furnace, such as tinkers use to melt their spelter; charcoal and dry chips fill it, so that a spark would suffice to kindle this furnace in a minute.

Not far from this collection of ugly instruments, putting one in mind of a torturer's kit of tools, there are some articles of defence and offence of a bygone age. A coat of mail, with links so flexible, close, and light, that it resembles steel tissue, hangs from a box beside iron cuishes and arm-pieces, in good condition, even to being properly fitted with straps. A mace, and two long three-cornered-headed pikes, with ash handles, strong, and light at the same time; spotted with lately-shed blood, complete the armory, modernized somewhat by the presence of two Tyrolese rifles, loaded and primed.

Along with this arsenal of murderous weapons and out-of-date instruments, is strangely mingled a collection of very different objects, being small glass-lidded boxes, full of rosaries, chaplets, medals, AGNUS DEI, holy water bottles, framed pictures of saints, etc., not to forget a goodly number of those chapbooks, struck off in Friburg on coarse bluish paper, in which you can hear about miracles of our own time, or "Jesus Christ's Letter to a true believer," containing awful predictions, as for the years 1831 and '32, about impious revolutionary France.

One of those canvas daubs, with which strolling showmen adorn their booths, hangs from a rafter, no doubt to prevent its being spoilt by too long rolling up. It bore the following legend:

"THE DOWNRIGHT TRUE AND MOST MEMORABLE CONVERSION OF IGNATIUS MOROK, KNOWN AS THE PROPHET, HAPPENING IN FRIBURG, 1828TH YEAR OF GRACE."

This picture, of a size larger than natural, of gaudy color, and in bad taste, is divided into three parts, each presenting an important phase in the life of the convert, surnamed "The Prophet." In the first, behold a long-bearded man, the hair almost white, with uncouth face, and clad in reindeer skin, like the Siberian savage. His black foreskin cap is topped with a raven's head; his features express terror. Bent forward in his sledge, which half-a-dozen huge tawny dogs draw over the snow, he is fleeing from the pursuit of a pack of foxes, wolves, and big bears, whose gaping jaws, and formidable teeth, seem quite capable of devouring man, sledge, and dogs, a hundred times over. Beneath this section, reads:

"IN 1810, MOROK, THE IDOLATER, FLED FROM WILD BEASTS."

In the second picture, Morok, decently clad in a catechumen's white gown kneels, with clasped hands, to a man who wears a white neckcloth, and flowing black robe. In a corner, a tall angel, of repulsive aspect, holds a trumpet in one hand, and flourishes a flaming sword with the other, while the words which follow flow out of his mouth, in red letters on a black ground:

"MOROK, THE IDOLATER, FLED FROM WILD BEASTS; BUT WILD BEASTS WILL FLEE FROM IGNATIUS MOROK, CONVERTED AND BAPTIZED IN FRIBURG."

Thus, in the last compartment, the new convert proudly, boastfully, and triumphantly parades himself in a flowing robe of blue; head up, left arm akimbo, right hand outstretched, he seems to scare the wits out of a multitude of lions, tigers, hyenas, and bears, who, with sheathed claws, and masked teeth, crouch at his feet, awestricken, and submissive.

Under this, is the concluding moral:

"IGNATIUS MOROK BEING CONVERTED, WILD BEASTS CROUCH BEFORE HIM."

Not far from this canvas are several parcels of halfpenny books, likewise from the Friburg press, which relate by what an astounding miracle Morok, the Idolater, acquired a supernatural power almost divine, the moment he was converted - a power which the wildest animal could not resist, and which was testified to every day by the lion tamer's performances, "given less to display his courage than to show his praise unto the Lord."

Through the trap-door which opens into the loft, reek up puffs of a rank, sour, penetrating odor. From time to time are heard sonorous growls and deep breathings, followed by a dull sound, as of great bodies stretching themselves heavily along the floor.

A man is alone in this loft. It is Morok, the tamer of wild beasts, surnamed the Prophet.

He is forty years old, of middle height, with lank limbs, and an exceedingly spare frame; he is wrapped in a long, blood-red pelisse, lined with black fur; his complexion, fair by nature is bronzed by the wandering life he has led from childhood; his hair, of that dead yellow peculiar to certain races of the Polar countries, falls straight and stiff down his shoulders; and his thin, sharp, hooked nose, and prominent cheek-bones, surmount a long beard, bleached almost to whiteness. Peculiarly marking the physiognomy of this man is the wide open eye, with its tawny pupil ever encircled by a rim of white. This fixed, extraordinary look, exercises a real fascination over animals - which, however, does not prevent the Prophet from also employing, to tame them, the terrible arsenal around him.

Seated at a table, he has just opened the false bottom of a box, filled with chaplets and other toys, for the use of the devout. Beneath this false bottom, secured by a secret lock, are several sealed envelopes, with no other address than a number, combined with a letter of the alphabet. The Prophet takes one of these packets, conceals it in the pocket of his pelisse, and, closing the secret fastening of the false bottom, replaces the box upon a shelf.

This scene occurs about four o'clock in the afternoon, in the White Falcon, the only hostelry in the little village of Mockern, situated near Leipsic, as you come from the north towards France.

After a few moments, the loft is shaken by a hoarse roaring from below.

"Judas! be quiet!" exclaims the Prophet, in a menacing tone, as he turns his head towards the trap door.

Another deep growl is heard, formidable as distant thunder.

"Lie down, Cain!" cries Morok, starting from his seat.

A third roar, of inexpressible ferocity, bursts suddenly on the ear.

"Death! Will you have done," cries the Prophet, rushing towards the trap door, and addressing a third invisible animal, which bears this hastly name.

Notwithstanding the habitual authority of his voice - notwithstanding his reiterated threats - the brute-tamer cannot obtain silence: on the contrary, the barking of several dogs is soon added to the roaring of the wild beasts. Morok seizes a pike, and approaches the ladder; he is about to descend, when he sees some one issuing from the aperture.

The new-comer has a brown, sun-burnt face; he wears a gray hat, bell crowned and broad-brimmed, with a short jacket, and wide trousers of green cloth; his dusty leathern gaiters show that he has walked some distance; a game-bag is fastened by straps to his back.

"The devil take the brutes!" cried he, as he set foot on the floor; "one would think they'd forgotten me in three days. Judas thrust his paw through the bars of his cage, and Death danced like a fury. They don't know me any more, it seems?"

This was said in German. Morok answered in the same language, but with a slightly foreign accent.

"Good or bad news, Karl?" he inquired, with some uneasiness.

"Good news."

"You've met them!"

"Yesterday; two leagues from Wittenberg."

"Heaven be praised!" cried Morok, clasping his hands with intense satisfaction.

"Oh, of course, 'tis the direct road from Russia to France, 'twas a thousand to one that we should find them somewhere between Wittenberg and Leipsic."

Eugene Sue

"And the description?"

"Very close: two young girls in mourning; horse, white; the old man has long moustache, blue forage-cap; gray topcoat and a Siberian dog at his heels."

"And where did you leave them?"

"A league hence. They will be here within the hour."

"And in this inn - since it is the only one in the village," said Morok, with a pensive air.

"And night drawing on," added Karl.

"Did you get the old man to talk?"

"Him! - you don't suppose it!"

"Why not?"

"Go, and try yourself."

"And for what reason?"

"Impossible."

"Impossible - why?"

"You shall know all about it. Yesterday, as if I had fallen in with them by chance, I followed them to the place where they stopped for the night. I spoke in German to the tall old man, accosting him, as is usual with wayfarers, 'Good-day, and a pleasant journey, comrade!' But, for an answer, he looked askant at me, and pointed with, the end of his stick to the other side of the road."

"He is a Frenchman, and, perhaps, does not understand German."

"He speaks it, at least as well as you; for at the inn I heard him ask the host for whatever he and the young girls wanted."

"And did you not again attempt to engage him in conversation?"

"Once only; but I met with such a rough reception, that for fear of making mischief, I did not try again. Besides, between ourselves, I can tell you this man has a devilish ugly look; believe me, in spite of his gray moustache, he looks so vigorous and resolute, though with no more flesh on him than a carcass, that I don't know whether he or my mate Giant Goliath, would have the best of it in a struggle. I know not your plans: only take care, master - take care!"

"My black panther of Java was also very vigorous and very vicious," said Morok, with a grim, disdainful, smile.

"What, Death? Yes; in truth; and she is vigorous and vicious as ever. Only to you she is almost mild."

"And thus I will break this tall old man; notwithstanding his strength and surliness."

"Humph! humph! be on your guard, master. You are clever, you are as brave as any one; but, believe me, you will never make a lamb out of the old wolf that will be here presently."

"Does not my lion, Cain - does not my tiger, Judas, crouch in terror before me?"

"Yes, I believe you there - because you have means -"

"Because I have faith: that is all - and it is all," said Morok, imperiously interrupting Karl, and accompanying these words with such a look, that the other hung his head and was silent.

"Why should not he whom the Lord upholds in his struggle with wild beasts, be also upheld in his struggle with men, when

Eugene Sue

those men are perverse and impious?" added the Prophet, with a triumphant, inspired air.

Whether from belief in his master's conviction, or from inability to engage in a controversy with him on so delicate a subject, Karl answered the Prophet, humbly: "you are wiser than I am, master; what you do must be well done."

"Did you follow this old man and these two young girls all day long?" resumed the Prophet, after a moment's silence.

"Yes; but at a distance. As I know the country well, I sometimes cut across a valley, sometimes over a hill, keeping my eye upon the road, where they were always to be seen. The last time I saw them, I was hid behind the water-mill by the potteries. As they were on the highway for this place, and night was drawing on, I quickened my pace to get here before them, and be the bearer of what you call good news."

"Very good - yes - very good: and you shall be rewarded; for if these people had escaped me -"

The Prophet started, and did not conclude the sentence. The expression of his face, and the tones of his voice, indicated the importance of the intelligence which had just been brought him.

"In truth," rejoined Karl, "it may be worth attending to; for that Russian courier, all plastered with lace, who came, without slacking bridle, from St. Petersburg to Leipsic, only to see you, rode so fast, perhaps, for the purpose -"

Morok abruptly interrupted Karl, and said:

"Who told you that the arrival of the courier had anything to do with these travellers? You are mistaken; you should only know what I choose to tell you."

"Well, master, forgive me, and let's say no more about it. So! I will get rid of my game-bag, and go help Goliath to feed the brutes, for their supper time draws near, if it is not already past. Does our big giant grow lazy, master?"

"Goliath is gone out; he must not know that you are returned; above all, the tall old man and the maidens must not see you here - it would make them suspect something."

"Where do you wish me to go, then?"

"Into the loft, at the end of the stable, and wait my orders; you may this night have to set out for Leipsic."

"As you please; I have some provisions left in my pouch, and can sup in the loft whilst I rest myself."

"Go."

"Master, remember what I told you. Beware of that old fellow with the gray moustache; I think he's devilish tough; I'm up to these things - he's an ugly customer - be on your guard!"

"Be quite easy! I am always on my guard," said Morok.

"Then good luck to you, master!" - and Karl, having reached the ladder, suddenly disappeared.

After making a friendly farewell gesture to his servant, the Prophet walked up and down for some time, with an air of deep meditation; then, approaching the box which contained the papers, he took out a pretty long letter, and read it over and over with profound attention. From time to time he rose and went to the closed window, which looked upon the inner court of the inn, and appealed to listen anxiously; for he waited with impatience the arrival of the three persons whose approach had just been announced to him.

CHAPTER II

THE TRAVELLERS

While the above scene was passing in the White Falcon at Mockern, the three persons whose arrival Morok was so anxiously expecting, travelled on leisurely in the midst of smiling meadows, bounded on one side by a river, the current of which turned a mill; and on the other by the highway leading to the village, which was situated on an eminence, at about a league's distance.

The sky was beautifully serene; the bubbling of the river, beaten by the mill-wheel and sparkling with foam, alone broke upon the silence of an evening profoundly calm. Thick willows, bending over the river, covered it with their green transparent shadow; whilst, further on, the stream reflected so splendidly the blue heavens and the glowing tints of the west, that, but for the hills which rose between it and the sky, the gold and azure of the water would have mingled in one dazzling sheet with the gold and azure of the firmament. The tall reeds on the bank bent their black velvet heads beneath the light breath of the breeze that rises at the close of day - for the sun was gradually sinking behind a broad streak of purple clouds, fringed with fire. The tinkling bells of a flock of sheep sounded from afar in the clear and sonorous air.

Along a path trodden in the grass of the meadow, two girls, almost children - for they had but just completed their fifteenth year - were riding on a white horse of medium size, seated upon a large saddle with a back to it, which easily took them both in, for their figures were slight and delicate.

A man of tall stature, with a sun-burnt face, and long gray moustache, was leading the horse by the bridle, and ever and anon turned towards the girls, with an air of solicitude at once respectful and paternal. He leaned upon a long staff; his still robust shoulders carried a soldier's knapsack; his dusty shoes, and step that began to drag a little, showed that he had walked a long way.

One of those dogs which the tribes of Northern Siberia harness to their sledges - a sturdy animal, nearly of the size, form, and hairy coat of the wolf - followed closely in the steps of the leader of this little caravan, never quitting, as it is commonly said, the heels of his master.

Nothing could be more charming than the group formed by the girls. One held with her left hand the flowing reins, and with her right encircled the waist of her sleeping sister, whose head reposed on her shoulder. Each step of the horse gave a graceful swaying to these pliant forms, and swung their little feet, which rested on a wooden ledge in lieu of a stirrup.

These twin sisters, by a sweet maternal caprice, had been called Rose and Blanche; they were now orphans, as might be seen by their sad mourning vestments, already much worn. Extremely, like in feature, and of the same size, it was necessary to be in the constant habit of seeing them, to distinguish one from the other. The portrait of her who slept not, might serve them for both of them; the only difference at the moment being, that Rose was awake and discharging for that day the duties of elder sister - duties thus divided between then, according to the fancy of their guide, who, being an old soldier of the empire, and a martinet, had judged fit thus to alternate obedience and command between the orphans.

Greuze would have been inspired by the sight of those sweet faces, coifed in close caps of black velvet, from beneath which

Eugene Sue

strayed a profusion of thick ringlets of a light chestnut color, floating down their necks and shoulders, and setting, as in a frame, their round, firm, rosy, satin like cheeks. A carnation, bathed in dew, is of no richer softness than their blooming lips; the wood violet's tender blue would appear dark beside the limpid azure of their large eyes, in which are depicted the sweetness of their characters, and the innocence of their age; a pure and white forehead, small nose, dimpled chin, complete these graceful countenances, which present a delightful blending of candor and gentleness.

You should have seen them too, when, on the threatening of rain or storm, the old soldier carefully wrapped them both in a large pelisse of reindeer fur, and pulled over their heads the ample hood of this impervious garment; then nothing could be more lovely than those fresh and smiling little faces, sheltered beneath the dark-colored cowl.

But now the evening was fine and calm; the heavy cloak hung in folds about the knees of the sisters, and the hood rested on the back of their saddle.

Rose, still encircling with her right arm the waist of her sleeping sister, contemplated her with an expression of ineffable tenderness, akin to maternal; for Rose was the eldest for the day, and an elder sister is almost a mother.

Not only, did the orphans idolize each other; but, by a psychological phenomenon, frequent with twins, they were almost always simultaneously affected; the emotion of one was reflected instantly in the countenance of the other; the same cause would make both of them start or blush, so closely did their young hearts beat in unison; all ingenuous joys, all bitter griefs were mutually felt, and shared in a moment between them.

In their infancy, simultaneously attacked by a severe illness, like two flowers on the same steam, they had drooped, grown pale, and languished together; but together also had they again found the pure, fresh hues of health.

Need it be said, that those mysterious, indissoluble links which united the twins, could not have been broken without striking a mortal blow at the existence of the poor children?

Thus the sweet birds called love-birds, only living in pairs, as if endowed with a common life, pine, despond, and die, when parted by a barbarous hand.

The guide of the orphans, a man of about fifty-five, distinguished by his military air and gait, preserved the immortal type of the warriors of the republic and the empire - some heroic of the people, who became, in one campaign, the first soldiers in the world - to prove what the people can do, have done, and will renew, when the rulers of their choice place in them confidence, strength, and their hope.

This soldier, guide of the sisters, and formerly a horse-grenadier of the Imperial Guard, had been nicknamed Dagobert. His grave, stern countenance was strongly marked; his long, gray, and thick moustache completely concealed his upper lip, and united with a large imperial, which almost covered his chin; his meagre cheeks, brick-colored, and tanned as parchment, were carefully shaven; thick eyebrows, still black, overhung and shaded his light blue eyes; gold ear-rings reached down to his white-edged military stock; his topcoat, of coarse gray cloth, was confined at the waist by a leathern belt; and a blue foraging cap, with a red tuft falling on his left shoulder, covered his bald head.

Once endowed with the strength of Hercules, and having still the heart of a lion - kind and patient, because he was courageous and strong - Dagobert, notwithstanding his rough exterior, evinced for his orphan charges an exquisite solicitude, a watchful kindness, and a tenderness almost maternal. Yes, motherly; for the heroism of affection dwells alike in the mother's heart and the soldiers.

Stoically calm, and repressing all emotion, the unchangeable coolness of Dagobert never failed him; and, though few were less given to drollery, he was now and then highly comic, by reason of the imperturbable gravity with which he did everything.

From time to time, as they journeyed on, Dagobert would turn to bestow a caress or friendly word on the good white home upon which the orphans were mounted. Its furrowed sides and long teeth betrayed a venerable age. Two deep scars, one on the flank and the other on the chest, proved that his horse had been present in hot battles; nor was it without an act of pride that he sometimes shook his old military bridle, the brass stud of which was still adorned with an embossed eagle. His pace was regular, careful, and steady; his coat sleek, and his bulk moderate; the abundant foam, which covered his bit, bore witness to that health which horses acquire by the constant, but not excessive, labor of a long journey, performed by short stages. Although he had been more than six months on the road, this excellent animal carried the orphans, with a tolerably heavy portmanteau fastened to the saddle, as freely as on the day they started.

If we have spoken of the excessive length of the horse's teeth - the unquestionable evidence of great age - it is chiefly because he often displayed them, for the sole purpose of acting up to his name (he was called Jovial), by playing a mischievous trick, of which the dog was the victim.

This latter, who, doubtless for the sake of contrast, was called Spoil-sport (Rabat-joie), being always at his master's heels, found himself within the reach of Jovial, who from time to time nipped him delicately by the nape of the neck, lifted him from the ground, and carried him thus for a moment. The dog, protected by his thick coat, and no doubt long accustomed to the practical jokes of his companion, submitted to all this with stoical complacency; save that, when he thought the jest had lasted long enough, he would turn his head and growl. Jovial understood him at the first hint, and hastened to set him down again. At other times, just to avoid monotony, Jovial would gently bite the knapsack of the soldier, who seemed, as well as the dog, to be perfectly accustomed to his pleasantries.

These details will give a notion of the excellent understanding that existed between the twin sisters, the old soldier, the horse, and the dog.

The little caravan proceeded on its ways anxious to reach, before night, the village of Mockern, which was now visible on the summit of a hill. Ever and anon, Dagobert looked around him, and seemed to be gathering up old recollections; by degrees, his countenance became clouded, and when he was at a little distance from the mill, the noise of which had arrested his attention, he stopped, and drew his long moustache several times between his finger and thumb, the only sign which revealed in him any strong and concentrated feeling.

Jovial, having stopped short behind his master, Blanche, awakened suddenly by the shock, raised her head; her first look sought her sister, on whom she smiled sweetly; then both exchanged glances of surprise, on seeing Dagobert motionless, with his hands clasped and resting on his long staff, apparently affected by some painful and deep emotion.

The orphans just chanced to be at the foot of a little mound, the summit of which was buried in the thick foliage of a huge oak, planted half way down the slope. Perceiving that Dagobert continued motionless and absorbed in thought, Rose leaned over her saddle, and, placing her little white hand on the shoulder of their guide, whose back was turned towards her, said to him, in a soft voice, "Whatever is the matter with you, Dagobert?"

The veteran turned; to the great astonishment of the sisters, they perceived a large tear, which traced its humid furrow down his tanned cheek, and lost itself in his thick moustache.

"You weeping - you!" cried Rose and Blanche together, deeply moved. "Tell us, we beseech, what is the matter?"

After a moments hesitation, the soldier brushed his horny hand across his eyes, and said to the orphans in a faltering voice, whilst he pointed to the old oak beside them: "I shall make you sad, my poor children: and yet what I'm going to tell you has something sacred in it. Well, eighteen years ago, on the eve of the great battle of Leipsic, I carried your father to this very tree. He had two sabre-cuts on the head, a musket ball in his shoulder; and it was here that he and I - who had got two thrust of a lance for my share - were taken prisoners; and by whom, worse luck? - why, a renegado! By a Frenchman - an emigrant marquis, then colonel in the service of Russia - and who afterwards - but one day you shall know all."

The veteran paused; then, pointing with his staff to the village of Mockern, he added: "Yes, yes, I can recognize the spot. Yonder are the heights where your brave father - who commanded us, and the Poles of the Guard - overthrew the Russian Cuirassiers, after having carried the battery. Ah, my children!" continued the soldier, with the utmost simplicity, "I wish you had, seen your brave father, at the head of our brigade of horse, rushing on in a desperate charge in the thick of a shower of shells! - There was nothing like it - not a soul so grand as he!"

Whilst Dagobert thus expressed, in his own way, his regrets and recollections, the two orphans - by a spontaneous movement, glided gently from the horse, and holding each other by the hand, went together to kneel at the foot of the old oak. And there, closely pressed in each other's arms, they began to weep; whilst the soldier, standing behind them, with his hands crossed on his long staff, rested his bald front upon it.

"Come, come you must not fret," said he softly, when, after a pause of a few minutes, he saw tears run down the blooming cheeks of Rose and Blanche, still on their knees. "Perhaps we may find General Simon in Paris," added he; "I will explain all that to you this evening at the inn. I purposely waited for this day, to tell you many things about your father; it was an idea of mine, because this day is a sort of anniversary."

"We weep because we think also of our mother," said Rose.

"Of our mother, whom we shall only see again in heaven," added Blanche.

The soldier raised the orphans, took each by the hand, and gazing from one to the other with ineffable affection, rendered still the more touching by the contrast of his rude features, "You must not give way thus, my children," said he; "it is true your mother was the best of women. When she lived in Poland, they called her the Pearl of Warsaw - it ought to have been the Pearl of the Whole World - for in the whole world you could not have found her match. No - no!"

The voice of Dagobert faltered; he paused, and drew his long gray moustache between finger and thumb, as was his habit. "Listen, my girls," he resumed, when he had mastered his emotion; "your mother could give you none but the best advice, eh?"

"Yes Dagobert."

"Well, what instructions did she give you before she died? To think often of her, but without grieving?"

"It is true; she told us than our Father in heaven, always good to poor mothers whose children are left on earth, would permit her to hear us from above," said Blanche.

"And that her eyes would be ever fixed upon us," added Rose.

And the two, by a spontaneous impulse, replete with the most touching grace, joined hands, raised their innocent looks to heaven, and exclaimed, with that beautiful faith natural to their age: "Is it not so, mother? - thou seest us? - thou hearest us?"

Eugene Sue

"Since your mother sees and hears you," said Dagobert, much moved, "do not grieve her by fretting. She forbade you to do so."

"You are right, Dagobert. We will not cry any more." - And the orphans dried their eyes.

Dagobert, in the opinion of the devout, would have passed for a very heathen. In Spain, he had found pleasure in cutting down those monks of all orders and colors, who, bearing crucifix in one hand, and poniard in the other, fought not for liberty - the Inquisition had strangled her centuries ago - but, for their monstrous privileges. Yet, in forty years, Dagobert had witnessed so many sublime and awful scenes - he had been so many times face to face with death - that the instinct of natural religion, common to every simple, honest heart, had always remained uppermost in his soul. Therefore, though he did not share in the consoling faith of the two sisters, he would have held as criminal any attempt to weaken its influence.

Seeing them this downcast, he thus resumed: "That's right, my pretty ones: I prefer to hear you chat as you did this morning and yesterday - laughing at times, and answering me when I speak, instead of being so much engrossed with your own talk. Yes, yes, my little ladies! you seem to have had famous secrets together these last two days - so, much the better, if it amuses you."

The sisters colored, and exchanged a subdued smile, which contrasted with the tears that yet filled their eyes, and Rose said to the soldier, with a little embarrassment. "No, I assure you, Dagobert, we talk of nothing in particular."

"Well, well; I don't wish to know it. Come, rest yourselves, a few moments more, and then we must start again; for it grows late, and we have to reach Mockern before night, so that we may be early on the road to-morrow."

"Have we still a long, long way to go?" asked Rose.

"What, to reach Paris? Yes, my children; some hundred days' march. We don't travel quick, but we get on; and we travel cheap, because we have a light purse. A closet for you, a straw mattress and a blanket at your door for me, with Spoil-sport on my feet, and a clean litter for old Jovial, these are our whole traveling expenses. I say nothing about food, because you two together don't eat more than a mouse, and I have learnt in Egypt and Spain to be hungry only when it suits."

"Not forgetting that, to save still more, you do all the cooking for us, and will not even let us assist."

"And to think, good Dagobert, that you wash almost every evening at our resting-place. As if it were not for us to -"

"You!" said the soldier, interrupting Blanche, "I, allow you to chap your pretty little hands in soap-suds! Pooh! don't a soldier on a campaign always wash his own linen? Clumsy as you see me, I was the best washerwoman in my squadron - and what a hand at ironing! Not to make a brag of it."

"Yes, yes - you can iron well - very well."

"Only sometimes, there will be a little singe," said Rose, smiling.

"Hah! when the iron is too hot. Zounds! I may bring it as near my cheek as I please; my skin is so tough that I don't feel the heat," said Dagobert, with imperturbable gravity.

"We are only jesting, good Dagobert!"

"Then, children, if you think that I know my trade as a washerwoman, let me continue to have your custom: it is cheaper; and, on a journey, poor people like us should save where we can, for we must, at all events, keep enough to reach Paris. Once there, our papers and the medal you wear will do the rest - I hope so, at least."

Eugene Sue

"This medal is sacred to us; mother gave it to us on her death-bed."

"Therefore, take great care that you do not lose it: see, from time to time, that you have it safe."

"Here it is," said Blanche, as she drew from her bosom a small bronze medal, which she wore suspended from her neck by a chain of the same material. The medal bore on its faces the following inscriptions:

Victim
of
L. C. D. J.
Pray for me!
Paris
February the, 13th, 1682.

At Paris.
Rue Saint Francois, No. 3,
In a century and a half
you will be.
February the 13th, 1832.
PRAY FOR ME!

"What does it mean, Dagobert?" resumed Blanche, as she examined the mournful inscriptions. "Mother was not able to tell us."

"We will discuss all that this evening; at the place where we sleep," answered Dagobert. "It grows late, let us be moving. Put up the medal carefully, and away! - We have yet nearly an hour's march to arrive at quarters. Come, my poor pets, once more look at the mound where your brave father fell - and then - to horse! to horse!"

The orphans gave a last pious glance at the spot which had recalled to their guide such painful recollections, and, with his aid, remounted Jovial.

This venerable animal had not for one moment dreamed of moving; but, with the consummate forethought of a veteran, he had made the best use of his time, by taking from that foreign soil a large contribution of green and tender grass, before the somewhat envious eyes of Spoil-sport, who had comfortably established himself in the meadow, with his snout protruding between his fore-paws. On the signal of departure, the dog resumed his post behind his master, and Dagobert, trying the ground with the end of his long staff, led the horse carefully along by the bridle, for the meadow was growing more and more marshy; indeed, after advancing a few steps, he was obliged to turn off to the left, in order to regain the high-road.

On reaching Mockern, Dagobert asked for the least expensive inn, and was told there was only one in the village - the White Falcon.

"Let us go then to the White Falcon," observed the soldier.

CHAPTER III

THE ARRIVAL

Already had Morok several times opened with impatience the window shutters of the loft, to look out upon the inn-yard, watching for the arrival of the orphans and the soldier. Not seeing them, he began once more to walk slowly up and down, with his head bent forward, and his arms folded on his bosom, meditating on the best means to carry out the plan he had conceived. The ideas which possessed his mind, were, doubtless, of a painful character, for his countenance grew even more gloomy than usual.

Notwithstanding his ferocious appearance, he was by no means deficient in intelligence. The courage displayed in his taming exercises (which he gravely attributed to his recent conversion), a solemn and mystical style of speech, and a hypocritical affectation of austerity, had given him a species of influence over the people he visited in his travels. Long before his conversion, as may well be supposed, Morok had been familiar with the habits of wild beasts. In fact born in the north of Siberia, he had been, from his boyhood, one of the boldest hunters of bears and reindeer; later, in 1810, he had abandoned this profession, to serve as guide to a Russian engineer, who was charged with an exploring expedition to the Polar regions. He afterwards followed him to St. Petersburg, and there, after some vicissitudes of fortune, Morok became one of the imperial couriers - these iron automata, that the least caprice of the despot hurls in a frail sledge through the immensity of the empire, from Persia to the Frozen Sea. For these men, who travel night and day, with the rapidity of lightning there are neither seasons nor obstacles, fatigues nor danger; living projectiles, they must either be broken to pieces, or reach the intended mark. One may conceive the boldness, the vigor, and the resignation, of men accustomed to such a life.

It is useless to relate here, by what series of singular circumstances Morok was induced to exchange his rough pursuit for another profession, and at last to enter, as catechumen, a religious house at Friburg; after which, being duly and properly converted, he began his nomadic excursions, with his menagerie of unknown origin.

Morok continued to walk up and down the loft. Night had come. The three persons whose arrival he so impatiently expected had not yet made their appearance. His walk became more and more nervous and irregular.

On a sudden he stopped abruptly; leaned his head towards the window; and listened. His ear was quick as a savage's.

"They are here!" he exclaimed and his fox like eye shone with diabolic joy. He had caught the sound of footsteps - a man's and a horse's. Hastening to the window-shutter of the loft, he opened it cautiously, and saw the two young girls on horseback, and the old soldier who served them as a guide, enter the inn-yard together.

The night had set in, dark and cloudy; a high wind made the lights flicker in the lanterns which were used to receive the new guests. But the description given to Morok had been so exact, that it was impossible to mistake them. Sure of his prey, he closed the window. Having remained in meditation for another quarter of an hour - for the purpose, no doubt, of thoroughly digesting his projects - he leaned over the aperture, from which projected the ladder, and called, "Goliath!"

"Master!" replied a hoarse voice.

"Come up to me."

"Here I am - just come from the slaughter-house with the meat."

The steps of the ladder creaked as an enormous head appeared on a level with the floor. The new-comer, who was more than six feet high, and gifted with herculean proportions, had been well-named Goliath. He was hideous. His squinting eyes were deep set beneath a low and projecting forehead; his reddish hair and beard, thick and coarse as horse-hair, gave his features a stamp of bestial ferocity; between his broad jaws, armed with teeth which resembled fangs, he held by one corner a piece of raw beef weighing ten or twelve pounds, finding it, no doubt, easier to carry in that fashion, whilst he used his hands to ascend the ladder, which bent beneath his weight.

At length the whole of this tall and huge body issued from the aperture. Judging by his bull-neck, the astonishing breadth of his chest and shoulders, and the vast bulk of his arms and legs, this giant need not have feared to wrestle single-handed with a bear. He wore an old pair of blue trousers with red stripes, faced with tanned sheep's-skin, and a vest, or rather cuirass, of thick leather, which was here and there slashed by the sharp claws of the animals.

When he was fairly on the floor, Goliath unclasped his fangs, opened his mouth, and let fall the great piece of beef, licking his blood-stained lips with greediness. Like many other mountebanks, this species of monster had began by eating raw meat at the fairs for the amusement of the public. Thence having gradually acquired a taste for this barbarous food, and uniting pleasure with profit, he engaged himself to perform the prelude to the exercises of Morok, by devouring, in the presence of the crowd, several pounds of raw flesh.

"My share and Death's are below stairs, and here are those of

Cain and Judas," said Goliath, pointing to the chunk of beef. "Where is the cleaver, that I may cut it in two? - No preference here - beast or man - every gullet must have it's own."

Then, rolling up one of the sleeves of his vest, he exhibited a fore-arm hairy as skin of a wolf, and knotted with veins as large as one's thumb.

"I say, master, where's the cleaver?" - He again began, as he cast round his eyes in search of that instrument. But instead of replying to this inquiry, the Prophet put many questions to his disciple.

"Were you below when just now some new travellers arrived at the inn?"

"Yes, master; I was coming from the slaughter-house."

"Who are these travellers?"

"Two young lasses mounted on a white horse, and an old fellow with a big moustache. But the cleaver? - my beasts are hungry and so am I - the cleaver!"

"Do you know where they have lodged these travellers?"

"The host took them to the far end of the court-yard."

"The building, which overlooks the fields?"

"Yes, master - but the cleaver -"

A burst of frightful roaring shook the loft, and interrupted Goliath.

"Hark to them!" he exclaimed; "hunger has driven the beasts wild. If I could roar, I should do as they do. I have never seen Judas and Cain as they are to-night; they leap in their cages as if they'd knock all to pieces. As for Death, her eyes shine more

Eugene Sue

than usual like candles - poor Death!"

"So these girls are lodged in the building at the end of the court-yard," resumed Morok, without attending to the observations of Goliath.

"Yes, yes - but in the devil's name, where is the cleaver? Since Karl went away I have to do all the work, and that makes our meals very late."

"Did the old man remain with the young girls?" asked Morok.

Goliath, amazed that, notwithstanding his importunities, his master should still appear to neglect the animals' supper, regarded the Prophet with an increase of stupid astonishment.

"Answer, you brute!"

"If I am a brute, I have a brute's strength," said Goliath, in a surly tone, "and brute against brute, I have not always come the worst off."

"I ask if the old man remained with the girls," repeated Morok.

"Well, then - no!" returned the giant. "The old man, after leading his horse to the stable, asked for a tub and some water, took his stand under the porch - and there - by the light of a lantern - he is washing out clothes. A man with a gray moustache! - paddling in soap-suds like a washerwoman - it's as if I were to feed canaries!" added Goliath shrugging his shoulders with disdain. "But now I've answered you, master, let me attend to the beasts' supper," - and, looking round for something, he added, "where is the cleaver?"

After a moment of thoughtful silence, the Prophet said to Goliath, "You will give no food to the beasts this evening."

At first the giant could not understand these words, the idea was so incomprehensible to him.

"What is your pleasure, master?" said he.

"I forbid you to give any food to the beasts this evening."

Goliath did not answer, but he opened wide his squinting eyes, folded his hands, and drew back a couple of steps.

"Well, dost hear me?" said Morok, with impatience. "Is it plain enough?"

"Not feed? when our meat is there, and supper is already three hours after time!" cried Goliath, with ever-increasing amazement.

"Obey, and hold your tongue."

"You must wish something bad to happen this evening. Hunger makes the beasts furious - and me also."

"So much the better!"

"It'll drive 'em mad."

"So much the better!"

"How, so much the better? - But -"

"It is enough!"

"But, devil take me, I am as hungry as the beasts!"

"Eat then - who prevents it? Your supper is ready, as you devour it raw."

"I never eat without my beasts, nor they without me."

"I tell you again, that, if you dare give any food to the beasts - I will turn you away."

Goliath uttered a low growl as hoarse as a bear's, and looked at the Prophet with a mixture of anger and stupefaction.

Morok, having given his orders, walked up and down the loft, appearing to reflect. Then, addressing himself to Goliath, who was still plunged in deep perplexity, he said to him.

"Do you remember the burgomaster's, where I went to get my passport signed? - To-day his wife bought some books and a chaplet."

"Yes," answered the giant shortly.

"Go and ask his servant if I may be sure to find the burgomaster early to-morrow morning."

"What for?"

"I may, perhaps, have something important to communicate; at all events, say that I beg him not to leave home without seeing me."

"Good! but may I feed the beasts before I go to the burgomaster's? - only the panther, who is most hungry? Come, master; only poor Death? just a little morsel to satisfy her; Cain and I and Judas can wait."

"It is the panther, above all, that I forbid you to feed. Yes, her, above all the rest."

"By the horns of the devil!" cried Goliath, "what is the matter with you to-day? I can make nothing of it. It is a pity that Karl's not here; he, being cunning, would help me to understand why you prevent the beasts from eating when they are hungry."

"You have no need to understand it."

"Will not Karl soon come back?"

"He has already come back."

"Where is he, then?"

"Off again."

"What can be going on here? There is something in the wind. Karl goes, and returns, and goes again, and -"

"We are not talking of Karl, but of you; though hungry as a wolf you are cunning as a fox, and, when it suits you, as cunning as Karl." And, changing on the sudden his tone and manner, Morok slapped the giant cordially on the shoulder.

"What! am I cunning?"

"The proof is, that there are ten florins to earn to-night - and you will be keen enough to earn them, I am sure."

"Why, on those terms, yes - I am awake," said the giant, smiling with a stupid, self-satisfied air. "What must I do for ten florins?"

"You shall see."

"Is it hard work?"

"You shall see. Begin by going to the burgomaster's - but first light the fire in that stove." He pointed to it with his finger.

"Yes, master," said Goliath, somewhat consoled for the delay of his supper by the hope of gaining ten florins.

"Put that iron bar in the stove," added the Prophet, "to make it red-hot."

"Yes, master."

Eugene Sue

"You will leave it there; go to the burgomaster's, and return here to wait for me."

"Yes, master.

"You will keep the fire up in the stove."

"Yes, master."

Morok took a step away, but recollecting himself, he resumed: "You say the old man is busy washing under the porch?"

"Yes, master."

"Forget nothing: the iron bar in the fire - the burgomaster - and return here to wait my orders." So saying, Morok descended by the trap-door and disappeared.

CHAPTER IV

MOROK and DAGOBERT

Goliath had not been mistaken, for Dagobert was washing with that imperturbable gravity with which he did everything else.

When we remember the habits of a soldier a-field, we need not be astonished at this apparent eccentricity. Dagobert only thought of sparing the scanty purse of the orphans, and of saving them all care and trouble; so every evening when they came to a halt he devoted himself to all sorts of feminine occupations. But he was not now serving his apprenticeship in these matters; many times, during his campaigns, he had industriously repaired the damage and disorder which a day of battle always brings to the garments of the soldier; for it is not enough to receive a sabre-cut - the soldier has also to mend his uniform; for the stroke which grazes the skin makes likewise a corresponding fissure in the cloth.

Therefore, in the evening or on the morrow of a hard-fought engagement, you will see the best soldiers (always distinguished by their fine military appearance) take from their cartridge-box or knapsack a housewife, furnished with needles, thread, scissors, buttons, and other such gear, and apply themselves to all kinds of mending and darning, with a zeal that the most industrious workwoman might envy.

We could not find a better opportunity to explain the name of

Dagobert, given to Francis Baudoin (the guide of the orphans) at a time when he was considered one of the handsomest and bravest horse-grenadiers of the Imperial Guard.

They had been fighting hard all day, without any decisive advantage. In the evening, the company to which our hero belonged was sent as outliers to occupy the ruins of a deserted village. Videttes being posted, half the troopers remained in saddle, whilst the others, having picketed their horses, were able to take a little rest. Our hero had charged valiantly that day without receiving any wound - for he counted as a mere memento the deep scratch on his thigh, which a kaiserlitz had inflicted in awkwardly attempting an upward thrust with the bayonet.

"You donkey! my new breeches!" the grenadier had exclaimed, when he saw the wide yawning rent, which he instantly avenged by running the Austrian through, with a thrust scientifically administered. For, if he showed a stoical indifference on the subject of injury to his skin, it was not so with regard to the ripping up of his best parade uniform.

He undertook, therefore, the same evening, at the bivouac, to repair this accident. Selecting his best needle and thread from the stores of his housewife, and arming his finger with a thimble, he began to play the tailor by the light of the watch-fire, having first drawn off his cavalry-boots, and also (if it must be confessed) the injured garment itself, which he turned the wrong side out the better to conceal the stitches.

This partial undress was certainly a breach of discipline: but the captain, as he went his round, could not forbear laughing at the sight of the veteran soldier, who, gravely seated, in a squatting position, with his grenadier cap on, his regimental coat on his back, his boots by his side, and his galligaskins in his lap, was sewing with all the coolness of a tailor upon his own shop-board.

Suddenly, a musket-shot is heard, and the videttes fall back upon the detachment, calling to arms. "To horse!" cries the captain, in a voice of thunder.

In a moment, the troopers are in their saddles, the unfortunate clothes mender having to lead the first rank; there is no time to turn the unlucky garment, so he slips it on, as well as he can, wrong side out, and leaps upon his horse, without even stopping to put on his boots.

A party of Cossacks, profiting by the cover of a neighboring wood, had attempted to surprise the detachment: the fight was bloody, and our hero foamed with rage, for he set much value on his equipments, and the day had been fatal to him. Thinking of his torn clothes and lost boots, he hacked away with more fury than ever; a bright moon illumined the scene of action, and his comrades were able to appreciate the brilliant valor of our grenadier, who killed two Cossacks, and took an officer prisoner, with his own hand.

After this skirmish, in which the detachment had maintained its position, the captain drew up his men to compliment them on their success, and ordered the clothes-mender to advance from the ranks, that he might thank him publicly for his gallant behavior. Our hero could have dispensed with this ovation, but he was not the less obliged to obey.

Judge of the surprise of both captain and troopers, when they saw this tall and stern-looking figure ride forward at a slow pace, with his naked feet in the stirrups, and naked legs pressing the sides of his charger.

The captain drew near in astonishment; but recalling the occupation of the soldier at the moment when the alarm was given, he understood the whole mystery. "Ha, my old comrade!" he exclaimed, "thou art like King Dagobert - wearing thy breeches inside out."

In spite of discipline, this joke of the captain's was received with peals of ill-repressed laughter. But our friend, sitting

Eugene Sue

upright in his saddle, with his left thumb pressing the well adjusted reins, and his sword-hilt carried close to his right thigh, made a half-wheel, and returned to his place in the ranks without changing countenance, after he had duly received the congratulations of his captain. From that day, Francis Baudoin received and kept the nickname of Dagobert.

Now Dagobert was under the porch of the inn, occupied in washing, to the great amazement of sundry beer-drinkers, who observed him with curious eyes from the large common room in which they were assembled.

In truth, it was a curious spectacle. Dagobert had laid aside his gray top-coat, and rolled up the sleeves of his shirt; with a vigorous hand, and good supply of soap, he was rubbing away at a wet handkerchief, spread out on the board, the end of which rested in a tub full of water. Upon his right arm, tattooed with warlike emblems in red and blue colors, two scars, deep enough to admit the finger, were distinctly visible. No wonder then, that, while smoking their pipes, and emptying their pots of beer, the Germans should display some surprise at the singular occupation of this tall, moustached, bald-headed old man, with the forbidding countenance - for the features of Dagobert assumed a harsh and grim expression, when he was no longer in presence of the two girls.

The sustained attention, of which he saw himself the object, began to put him out of patience, for his employment appeared to him quite natural. At this moment, the Prophet entered the porch, and, perceiving the soldier, eyed him attentively for several seconds; then approaching, he said to him in French, in a rather sly tone: "It would seem, comrade, that you have not much confidence in the washerwomen of Mockern?"

Dagobert, without discontinuing his work, half turned his head with a frown, looked askant at the Prophet, and made him no answer.

Astonished at this silence, Morok resumed: "If I do not deceive myself, you are French, my fine fellow. The words on your arm prove it, and your military air stamps you as an old soldier of the Empire. Therefore I find, that, for a hero, you have taken rather late to wear petticoats."

Dagobert remained mute, but he gnawed his moustache, and plied the soap, with which he was rubbing the linen, in a most hurried, not to say angry style; for the face and words of the beast-tamer displeased him more than he cared to show. Far from being discouraged, the Prophet continued: "I am sure, my fine fellow, that you are neither deaf nor dumb; why, then, will you not answer me?"

Losing all patience, Dagobert turned abruptly round, looked Morok full in the face, and said to him in a rough voice: "I don't know you: I don't wish to know you! Chain up your curb!" And he betook himself again to his washing.

"But we may make acquaintance. We can drink a glass of Rhine-wine together, and talk of our campaigns. I also have seen some service, I assure you; and that, perhaps, will induce you to be more civil."

The veins on the bald forehead of Dagobert swelled perceptibly; he saw in the look and accent of the man, who thus obstinately addressed him, something designedly provoking; still he contained himself.

"I ask you, why should you not drink a glass of wine with me - we could talk about France. I lived there a long time; it is a fine country; and when I meet Frenchmen abroad, I feel sociable - particularly when they know how to use the soap as well as you do. If I had a housewife I'd send her to your school."

The sarcastic meaning was no longer disguised; impudence and bravado were legible in the Prophet's looks. Thinking that, with such an adversary, the dispute might become serious,

Eugene Sue

Dagobert, who wished to avoid a quarrel at any price, carried off his tub to the other end of the porch, hoping thus to put an end to the scene which was a sore trial of his temper. A flash of joy lighted up the tawny eyes of the brute-tamer. The white circle, which surrounded the pupil seemed to dilate. He ran his crooked fingers two or three times through his yellow beard, in token of satisfaction; then he advanced slowly towards the soldier, accompanied byseveral idlers from the common-room.

Notwithstanding his coolness, Dagobert, amazed and incensed at the impudent pertinacity of the Prophet, was at first disposed to break the washing-board on his head; but, remembering the orphans, he thought better of it.

Folding his arms upon his breast, Morok said to him, in a dry and insolent tone: "It is very certain you are not civil, my man of suds!" Then, turning to the spectators, he continued in German: "I tell this Frenchman, with his long moustache, that he is not civil. We shall see what answer he'll make. Perhaps it will be necessary to give him a lesson. Heaven preserve me from quarrels!" he added, with mock compunction; "but the Lord has enlightened me - I am his creature, and I ought to make his work respected."

The mystical effrontery of this peroration was quite to the taste of the idlers; the fame of the Prophet had reached Mockern, and, as a performance was expected on the morrow, this prelude much amused the company. On hearing the insults of his adversary, Dagobert could not help saying in the German language: "I know German. Speak in German - the rest will understand you."

New spectators now arrived, and joined the first comers; the adventure had become exciting, and a ring was formed around the two persons most concerned.

The Prophet resumed in German: "I said that you were not civil, and I now say you are grossly rude. What do you answer to that?"

"Nothing!" said Dagobert, coldly, as he proceeded to rinse out another piece of linen.

"Nothing!" returned Morok; "that is very little. I will be less brief, and tell you, that, when an honest man offers a glass of wine civilly to a stranger, that stranger has no right to answer with insolence, and deserves to be taught manners if he does so."

Great drops of sweat ran down Dagobert's forehead and cheeks; his large imperial was incessantly agitated by nervous trembling - but he restrained himself. Taking, by two of the corners, the handkerchief which he had just dipped in the water, he shook it, wrung it, and began to hum to himself the burden of the old camp ditty:

> "Out of Tirlemont's flea-haunted den,
> We ride forth next day of the sen,
> With sabre in hand, ah!
> Good-bye to Amanda," etc.

The silence to which Dagobert had condemned himself, almost choked him; this song afforded him some relief.

Morok, turning towards the spectators, said to them, with an air of hypocritical restraint: "We knew that the soldiers of Napoleon were pagans, who stabled their horses in churches, and offended the Lord a hundred times a day, and who, for their sins, were justly drowned in the Beresino, like so many Pharaohs; but we did not know that the Lord, to punish these miscreants, had deprived them of courage - their single gift. Here is a man, who has insulted, in me, a creature favored by divine grace, and who affects not to understand that I require an apology; or else -"

"What?" said Dagobert, without looking at the Prophet.

"Or you must give me satisfaction! - I have already told you that I have seen service. We shall easily find somewhere a couple of swords, and to morrow morning, at peep of day, we can meet behind a wall, and show the color of our blood - that is, if you have any in your veins!"

This challenge began to frighten the spectators, who were not prepared for so tragical a conclusion.

"What, fight? - a very, fine idea!" said one. "To get yourself both locked up in prison: the laws against duelling are strict."

"Particularly with relation to strangers or nondescripts," added another. "If they were to find you with arms in your hands, the burgomaster would shut you up in jail, and keep you there two or three months before trial."

"Would you be so mean as to denounce us?" asked Morok.

"No, certainly not," cried several; "do as you like. We are only giving you a friendly piece of advice, by which you may profit, if you think fit."

"What care I for prison?" exclaimed the Prophet. "Only give me a couple of swords, and you shall see to-morrow morning if I heed what the burgomaster can do or say."

"What would you do with two swords?" asked Dagobert, quietly.

"When you have one in your grasp, and I one in mine, you'd see. The Lord commands us to have a care of his honor!"

Dagobert shrugged his shoulders, made a bundle of his linen in his handkerchief, dried his soap, and put it carefully into a little oil-silk bag - then, whistling his favorite air of Tirlemont, moved to depart.

The Prophet frowned; he began to fear that his challenge would not be accepted. He advanced a step or so to encounter Dagobert, placed himself before him, as if to intercept his passage, and, folding his arms, and scanning him from head to foot with bitter insolence, said to him: "So! an old soldier of that arch-robber, Napoleon, is only fit for a washerwoman, and refuses to fight!"

"Yes, he refuses to fight," answered Dagobert, in a firm voice, but becoming fearfully pale. Never, perhaps, had the soldier given to his orphan charge such a proof of tenderness and devotion. For a man of his character to let himself be insulted with impunity, and refuse to fight - the sacrifice was immense.

"So you are a coward - you are afraid of me - and you confess it?"

At these words Dagobert made, as it were, a pull upon himself - as if a sudden thought had restrained him the moment he was about to rush on the Prophet. Indeed, he had remembered the two maidens, and the fatal hindrance which a duel, whatever might be the result, would occasion to their journey. But the impulse of anger, though rapid, had been so significant - the expression of the stern, pale face, bathed in sweat, was so daunting, that the Prophet and the spectators drew back a step.

Profound silence reigned for some seconds, and then, by a sudden reaction, Dagobert seemed to have gained the general interest. One of the company said to those near him; "This man is clearly not a coward."

"Oh, no! certainly not."

"It sometimes requires more courage to refuse a challenge than to accept one."

"After all the Prophet was wrong to pick a quarrel about nothing - and with a stranger, too."

"Yes, for a stranger, if he fought and was taken up, would have a good long imprisonment."

Eugene Sue

"And then, you see," added another, "he travels with two young girls. In such a position, ought a man to fight about trifles? If he should be killed or put in prison, what would become of them, poor children?"

Dagobert turned towards the person who had pronounced these last words. He saw a stout fellow, with a frank and simple countenance; the soldier offered him his hand, and said with emotion:

"Thank you, sir."

The German shook cordially the hand, which Dagobert had proffered, and, holding it still in his own, he added: "Do one thing, sir - share a bowl of punch with us. We will make that mischief-making Prophet acknowledge that he has been too touchy, and he shall drink to your health."

Up to this moment the brute-tamer, enraged at the issue of this scene, for he had hoped that the soldier would accept his challenge, looked on with savage contempt at those who had thus sided against him. But now his features gradually relaxed; and, believing it useful to his projects to hide his disappointment, he walked up to the soldier, and said to him, with a tolerably good grace: "Well, I give way to these gentlemen. I own I was wrong. Your frigid air had wounded me, and I was not master of myself. I repeat, that I was wrong," he added, with suppressed vexation; "the Lord commands humility - and - I beg your pardon."

This proof of moderation and regret was highly appreciated and loudly applauded by the spectators. "He asks your pardon; you cannot expect more, my brave fellow?" said one of them, addressing Dagobert. "Come, let us all drink together; we make you this offer frankly - accept it in the same spirit."

"Yes, yes; accept it, we beg you, in the name of your pretty little girls," said the stout man, hoping to decide Dagobert by this argument.

"Many thanks, gentlemen," replied he, touched by the hearty advances of the Germans; "you are very worthy people. But, when one is treated, he must offer drink in return."

"Well, we will accept it - that's understood. Each his turn, and all fair. We will pay for the first bowl, you for the second."

"Poverty is no crime," answered Dagobert; "and I must tell you honestly that I cannot afford to pay for drink. We have still a long journey to go, and I must not incur any useless expenses."

The soldier spoke these words with such firm, but simple dignity, that the Germans did not venture to renew their offer, feeling that a man of Dagobert's character could not accept it without humiliation.

"Well, so much the worse," said the stout man. "I should have liked to clink glasses with you. Good-night, my brave trooper! - Good-night - for it grows late, and mine host of the Falcon will soon turn us out of doors."

"Good-night, gentlemen," replied Dagobert, as he directed his steps towards the stable, to give his horse a second allowance of provender.

Morok approached him, and said in a voice even more humble than before: "I have acknowledged my error, and asked your pardon. You have not answered me; do you still bear malice?"

"If ever I meet you," said the veteran, in a suppressed and hollow tone, "when my children have no longer need of me, I will just say two words to you, and they will not be long ones."

Then he turned his back abruptly on the Prophet, who walked slowly out of the yard.

The inn of the White Falcon formed a parallelogram. At one end rose the principal dwelling; at the other was a range of buildings, which contained sundry chambers, let at a low price to the poorer sort of travellers; a vaulted passage opened a way through this latter into the country; finally, on either side of the court-yard were sheds and stables, with lofts and garrets erected over them.

Dagobert, entering one of these stables, took from off a chest the portion of oats destined for his horse, and, pouring it into a winnowing basket, shook it as he approached Jovial.

To his great astonishment, his old travelling companion did not respond with a joyous neigh to the rustle of the oats rattling on the wicker work. Alarmed, he called Jovial with a friendly voice; but the animal, instead of turning towards his master a look of intelligence, and impatiently striking the ground with his fore-feet, remained perfectly motionless.

More and more surprised, the soldier went up to him. By the dubious light of a stable-lantern, he saw the poor animal in an attitude which implied terror - his legs half bent, his head stretched forward, his ears down, his nostrils quivering; he had drawn tight his halter, as if he wished to break it, in order to get away from the partition that supported his rack and manger; abundant cold-sweat had speckled his hide with bluish stains, and his coat altogether looked dull and bristling, instead of standing out sleek and glossy from the dark background of the stable; lastly, from time to time, his body shook with convulsive starts.

"Why, old Jovial!" said the soldier, as he put down the basket, in order to soothe his horse with more freedom, "you are like thy master - afraid! - Yes," he added with bitterness, as he thought of the offence he had himself endured, "you are afraid - though no coward in general."

Notwithstanding the caresses and the voice of his master, the horse continued to give signs of terror; he pulled somewhat less violently at his halter, and approaching his nostrils to the hand of Dagobert, sniffed audibly, as if he doubted it were he.

"You don't know me!" cried Dagobert. "Something extraordinary must be passing here."

The soldier looked around him with uneasiness. It was a large stable, faintly lighted by the lantern suspended from the roof, which was covered with innumerable cobwebs; at the further end, separated from Jovial by some stalls with bars between, were the three strong, black, horses of the brute-tamer - as tranquil as Jovial was frightened.

Dagobert, struck with this singular contrast, of which he was soon to have the explanation, again caressed his horse; and the animal, gradually reassured by his master's presence, licked his hands, rubbed his head against him, uttered a low neigh, and gave him his usual tokens of affection.

"Come, come, this is how I like to see my old Jovial!" said Dagobert, as he took up the winnowing-basket, and poured its contents into the manger. "Now eat with a good appetite, for we have a long day's march tomorrow; and, above all, no more of these foolish fears about nothing! If thy comrade, Spoilsport, was here, he would keep you in heart; but he is along with the children, and takes care of them in my absence. Come, eat! Instead of staring at me in that way."

But the horse, having just touched the oats with his mouth, as if in obedience to his master, returned to them no more, and began to nibble at the sleeve of Dagobert's coat.

"Come, come, my poor Jovial! there is something the matter with you. You have generally such a good appetite, and now you leave your corn. 'Tis the first time this has happened since our departure," said the soldier, who was now growing seriously uneasy, for the issue of his journey greatly depended on the health and vigor of his horse.

Just then a frightful roaring, so near that it seemed to come from the stable in which they were, gave so violent a shock to Jovial, that with one effort he broke his halter, leaped over the bar that marked his place, and rushing at the open door, escaped into the court-yard.

Dagobert had himself started at the suddenness of this wild and fearful sound, which at once explained to him the cause of his horse's terror. The adjoining stable was occupied by the itinerant menagerie of the brute-tamer, and was only separated by the partition, which supported the mangers. The three horses of the Prophet, accustomed to these howlings, had remained perfectly quiet.

"Good!" said the soldier, recovering himself; "I understand it now. Jovial has heard another such roar before, and he can scent the animals of that insolent scoundrel. It is enough to frighten him," added he, as he carefully collected the oats from the manger; "once in another stable, and there must be others in this place, he will no longer leave his peck, and we shall be able to start early to-morrow morning!"

The terrified horse, after running and galloping about the yard, returned at the voice of the soldier, who easily caught him by the broken halter; and a hostler, whom Dagobert asked if there was another vacant stable, having pointed out one that was only intended for a single animal, Jovial was comfortably installed there.

When delivered from his ferocious neighbors, the horse became tranquil as before, and even amused himself much at the expense of Dagobert's top coat, which, thanks to his tricks, might have afforded immediate occupation for his master's needle, if the latter had not been fully engaged in admiring the eagerness with which Jovial dispatched his provender. Completely reassured on his account, the soldier shut the door of the stable, and proceeded to get his supper as quickly as possible, in order to rejoin the orphans, whom he reproached himself with having left so long.

CHAPTER V

ROSE AND BLANCHE

The orphans occupied a dilapidated chamber in one of the most remote wings of the inn, with a single window opening upon the country. A bed without curtains, a table, and two chairs, composed the more than modest furniture of this retreat, which was now lighted by a lamp. On the table, which stood near the window, was deposited the knapsack of the soldier.

The great Siberian dog, who was lying close to the door, had already twice uttered a deep growl, and turned his head towards the window - but without giving any further affect to this hostile manifestation.

The two sisters, half recumbent in their bed, were clad in long white wrappers, buttoned at the neck and wrists. They wore no caps, but their beautiful chestnut hair was confined at the temples by a broad piece of tape, so that it might not get tangled during the night. These white garments, and the white fillet that like a halo encircled their brows, gave to their fresh and blooming faces a still more candid expression.

The orphans laughed and chatted, for, in spite of some early sorrows, they still retained the ingenuous gayety of their age. The remembrance of their mother would sometimes make them sad, but this sorrow had in it nothing bitter; it was rather a sweet melancholy, to be sought instead of shunned. For them, this adored mother was not dead - she was only absent.

Almost as ignorant as Dagobert, with regard to devotional exercises, for in the desert where they had lived there was neither church nor priest, their faith, as was already said, consisted in this - that God, just and good, had so much pity for the poor mothers whose children were left on earth, that he allowed them to look down upon them from highest heaven - to see them always, to hear them always, and sometimes to send fair guardian angels to protect therein. Thanks to this guileless illusion, the orphans, persuaded that their mother incessantly watched over them, felt, that to do wrong would be to afflict her, and to forfeit the protection of the good angels. - This was the entire theology of Rose and Blanche - a creed sufficient for such pure and loving souls.

Now, on the evening in question, the two sisters chatted together whilst waiting for Dagobert. Their theme interested them much, for, since some days, they had a secret, a great secret, which often quickened the beatings of their innocent hearts, often agitated their budding bosoms, changed to bright scarlet the roses on their cheeks, and infused a restless and dreamy langour into the soft blue of their large eyes.

Rose, this evening, occupied the edge of the couch, with her rounded arms crossed behind her head, which was half turned towards her sister; Blanche, with her elbow resting on the bolster, looked at her smilingly, and said: "Do you think he will come again to-night?"

"Oh, yes! certainly. He promised us yesterday."

"He is so good, he would not break his promise."

"And so handsome, with his long fair curls."

"And his name - what a charming name! - How well it suits his face."

"And what a sweet smile and soft voice, when he says to us, taking us by the hand: 'My children, bless God that he has given you one soul. What others seek elsewhere, you will find in yourselves.'"

"'Since your two hearts,' he added, 'only make one.'"

"What pleasure to remember his words, sister!"

"We are so attentive! When I see you listening to him, it is as if I saw myself, my dear little mirror!" said Rose, laughing, and kissing her sister's forehead. "Well - when he speaks, your - or rather our eyes - are wide, wide open, our lips moving as if we repeated every word after him. It is no wonder we forget nothing that he says."

"And what he says is so grand, so noble, and generous."

"Then, my sister, as he goes on talking, what good thoughts rise within us! If we could but always keep them in mind."

"Do not be afraid! they will remain in our hearts, like little birds in their mother's nests."

"And how lucky it is, Rose, that he loves us both at the same time!"

"He could not do otherwise, since we have but one heart between us."

"How could he love Rose, without loving Blanche?"

"What would have become of the poor, neglected one?"

"And then again he would have found it so difficult to choose."

"We are so much like one another."

"So, to save himself that trouble," said Rose, laughing, "he has chosen us both."

"And is it not the best way? He is alone to love us; we are two together to think of him."

"Only he must not leave us till we reach Paris."

"And in Paris, too - we must see him there also."

"Oh, above all at Paris; it will be good to have him with us - and Dagobert, too - in that great city. Only think, Blanche, how beautiful it must be."

"Paris! - it must be like a city all of gold."

"A city, where every one must be happy, since it is so beautiful."

"But ought we, poor orphans, dare so much as to enter it? How people will look at us!"

"Yes - but every one there is happy, every one must be good also."

"They will love us."

"And, besides, we shall be with our friend with the fair hair and blue eyes."

"He has yet told us nothing of Paris."

"He has not thought of it; we must speak to him about it this very night."

"If he is in the mood for talking. Often you know, he likes best to gaze on us in silence - his eyes on our eyes."

"Yes. In those moments, his look recalls to me the gaze of our dear mother."

"And, as she sees it all, how pleased she must be at what has happened to us!"

"Because, when we are so much beloved, we must, I hope, deserve it."

"See what a vain thing it is!" said Blanche, smoothing with her slender fingers the parting of the hair on her sister's forehead.

After a moment's reflection, Rose said to her: "Don't you think we should relate all this to Dagobert?"

"If you think so, let us do it."

"We tell him everything, as we told everything to mother. Why should we conceal this from him?"

"Especially as it is something which gives us so much pleasure."

"Do you not find that, since we have known our friend, our hearts beat quicker and stronger?"

"Yes, they seem to be more full."

"The reason why is plain enough; our friend fills up a good space in them."

"Well, we will do best to tell Dagobert what a lucky star ours is."

"You are right -" At this moment the dog gave another deep growl.

"Sister," said Rose, as she pressed closer to Blanche, "there is the dog growling again. What can be the matter with him?"

Eugene Sue

"Spoil-sport, do not growl! Come hither," said Blanche, striking with her little hand on the side of the bed.

The dog rose, again growled deeply, and came to lay his great, intelligent looking head on the counterpane, still obstinately casting a sidelong glance at the window; the sisters bent over him to pat his broad forehead, in the centre of which was a remarkable bump, the certain sign of extreme purity of race.

"What makes you growl so, Spoil-sport?" said Blanche, pulling him gently by the ears - "eh, my good dog?"

"Poor beast! he is always so uneasy when Dagobert is away."

"It is true; one would think he knows that he then has a double charge over us."

"Sister, it seems to me, Dagobert is late in coming to say good-night."

"No doubt he is attending to Jovial."

"That makes me think that we did not bid good-night to dear old Jovial.

"I am sorry for it."

"Poor beast! he seems so glad when he licks our hands. One would think that he thanked us for our visit."

"Luckily, Dagobert will have wished him good-night for us."

"Good Dagobert! he is always thinking of us. How he spoils us! We remain idle, and he has all the trouble."

"How can we prevent it?"

"What a pity that we are not rich, to give him a little rest."

"We rich! Alas, my sister! we shall never be anything but poor orphans."

"Oh, there's the medal!"

"Doubtless, there is some hope attached to it, else we should not have made this long journey."

"Dagobert has promised to tell us all, this evening."

She was prevented from continuing, for two of the window-panes flew to pieces with a loud crash.

The orphans, with a cry of terror, threw themselves into each other's arms, whilst the dog rushed towards the window, barking furiously.

Pale, trembling, motionless with affright, clasping each other in a close embrace, the two sisters held their breath; in their extreme fear, they durst not even cast their eyes in the direction of the window. The dog, with his forepaws resting on the sill, continued to bark with violence.

"Alas! what can it be?" murmured the orphans. "And Dagobert not here!"

"Hark!" cried Rose, suddenly seizing Blanche by the arm; "hark! - some one coming up the stairs!"

"Good heaven! it does not sound like the tread of Dagobert. Do you not hear what heavy footsteps?"

"Quick! come, Spoil-sport, and defend us!" cried the two sisters at once, in an agony of alarm.

The boards of the wooden staircase really creaked beneath the weight of unusually heavy footsteps, and a singular kind of rustling was heard along the thin partition that divided the chamber from the landing-place. Then a ponderous mass, falling against the door of the room, shook it violently; and the girls, at the very height of terror, looked at each other without the power of speech.

The door opened. It was Dagobert.

At the sight of him Rose and Blanche joyfully exchanged a kiss, as if they had just escaped from a great danger.

"What is the matter? why are you afraid?" asked the soldier in surprise.

"Oh, if you only knew!" said Rose, panting as she spoke, for both her own heart and her sister's beat with violence.

"If you knew what has just happened! We did not recognize your footsteps - they seemed so heavy - and then that noise behind the partition!"

"Little frightened doves that you are! I could not run up the stairs like a boy of fifteen, seeing that I carried my bed upon my back - a straw mattress that I have just flung down before your door, to sleep there as usual."

"Bless me! how foolish we must be, sister, not to have thought of that!" said Rose, looking at Blanche. And their pretty faces, which had together grown pale, together resumed their natural color.

During this scene the dog, still resting against the window, did not cease barking a moment.

"What makes Spoil-sport bark in that direction, my children?" said the soldier.

"We do not know. Two of our windowpanes have just been broken. That is what first frightened us so much."

Without answering a word Dagobert flew to the window,

opened it quickly, pushed back the shutter, and leaned out.

He saw nothing; it was a dark night. He listened; but heard only the moaning of the wind.

"Spoil-sport," said he to his dog, pointing to the open window, "leap out, old fellow, and search!" The faithful animal took one mighty spring and disappeared by the window, raised only about eight feet above the ground.

Dagobert, still leaning over, encouraged his dog with voice and gesture: "Search, old fellow, search! If there is any one there, pin him - your fangs are strong - and hold him fast till I come."

But Spoil-sport found no one. They heard him go backwards and forwards, snuffing on every side, and now and then uttering a low cry like a hound at fault.

"There is no one, my good dog, that's clear, or you would have had him by the throat ere this." Then, turning to the maidens, who listened to his words and watched his movements with uneasiness: "My girls," said he, "how were these panes broken? Did you not remark?"

"No, Dagobert; we were talking together when we heard a great crash, and then the glass fell into the room."

"It seemed to me," added Rose, "as if a shutter had struck suddenly against the window."

Dagobert examined the shutter, and observed a long movable hook, designed to fasten it on the inside.

"It blows hard," said he; "the wind must have swung round the shutter, and this hook broke the window. Yes, yes; that is it. What interest could anybody have to play such a sorry trick?" Then, speaking to Spoil sport, he asked, "Well, my good fellow, is there no one?"

Eugene Sue

The dog answered by a bark, which the soldier no doubt understood as a negative, for he continued: "Well, then, come back! Make the round - you will find some door open - you are never at a loss."

The animal followed this advice. After growling for a few seconds beneath the window, he set off at a gallop to make the circuit of the buildings, and come back by the court-yard.

"Be quite easy, my children!" said the soldier, as he again drew near the orphans; "it was only the wind."

"We were a good deal frightened," said Rose.

"I believe you. But now I think of it, this draught is likely to give you cold." And seeking to remedy this inconvenience, he took from a chair the reindeer pelisse, and suspended it from the spring-catch of the curtainless window, using the skirts to stop up as closely as possible the two openings made by the breaking of the panes.

"Thanks, Dagobert, how good you are! We were very uneasy at not seeing you."

"Yes, you were absent longer than usual. But what is the matter with you?" added Rose, only just then perceiving that his countenance was disturbed and pallid, for he was still under the painful influence of the brawl with Morok; "how pale you are!"

"Me, my pets? - Oh, nothing."

"Yes, I assure you, your countenance is quite changed. Rose is right."

"I tell you there is nothing the matter," answered the soldier, not without some embarrassment, for he was little used to deceive; till, finding an excellent excuse for his emotion, he added: "If I do look at all uncomfortable, it is your fright that has made me so, for indeed it was my fault."

"Your fault!"

"Yes; for if I had not lost so much time at supper, I should have been here when the window was broken, and have spared you the fright."

"Anyhow, you are here now, and we think no more of it."

"Why don't you sit down?"

"I will, my children, for we have to talk together," said Dagobert, as he drew a chair close to the head of the bed.

"Now tell me, are you quite awake?" he added, trying to smile in order to reassure them. "Are those large eyes properly open?"

"Look, Dagobert!" cried the two girls, smiling in their turn, and opening their blue eyes to the utmost extent.

"Well, well," said the soldier, "they are yet far enough, from shutting; besides, it is only nine o'clock."

"We also have something to tell, Dagobert," resumed Rose, after exchanging glances with her sister.

"Indeed!"

"A secret to tell you."

"A secret?"

"Yes, to be sure."

"Ah, and a very great secret!" added Rose, quite seriously.

"A secret which concerns us both," resumed Blanche.

"Faith! I should think so. What concerns the one always concerns the other. Are you not always, as the saying goes, 'two faces under one hood?'"

"Truly, how can it be otherwise, when you put our heads under the great hood of your pelisse?" said Rose, laughing.

"There they are again, mocking-birds! One never has the last word with them. Come, ladies, your secret, since a secret there is."

"Speak, sister," said Rose.

"No, miss, it is for you to speak. You are to-day on duty, as eldest, and such an important thing as telling a secret like that you talk of belongs of right to the elder sister. Come, I am listening to you," added the soldier, as he forced a smile, the better to conceal from the maidens how much he still felt the unpunished affronts of the brute tamer.

It was Rose (who, as Dagobert said, was doing duty as eldest) that spoke for herself and for her sister.

CHAPTER VI

THE SECRET

"First of all, good Dagobert," said Rose, in a gracefully caressing manner, "as we are going to tell our secret - you must promise not to scold us."

"You will not scold your darlings, will you?" added Blanche, in a no less coaxing voice.

"Granted!" replied Dagobert gravely; "particularly as I should not well know how to set about it - but why should I scold you."

"Because we ought perhaps to have told you sooner what we are going to tell you."

"Listen, my children," said Dagobert sententiously, after reflecting a moment on this case of conscience; "one of two things must be. Either you were right, or else you were wrong, to hide this from me. If you were right, very well; if you were wrong, it is done: so let's say no more about it. Go on - I am all attention."

Completely reassured by this luminous decision, Rose resumed, while she exchanged a smile with her sister.

"Only think, Dagobert; for two successive nights we have had a visitor."

Eugene Sue

"A visitor!" cried the soldier, drawing himself up suddenly in his chair.

"Yes, a charming visitor - he is so very fair."

"Fair - the devil!" cried Dagobert, with a start.

"Yes, fair - and with blue eyes," added Blanche.

"Blue eyes - blue devils!" and Dagobert again bounded on his seat.

"Yes, blue eyes - as long as that," resumed Rose, placing the tip of one forefinger about the middle of the other.

"Zounds! they might be as long as that," said the veteran, indicating the whole length of his term from the elbow, "they might be as long as that, and it would have nothing to do with it. Fair, and with blue eyes. Pray what may this mean, young ladies?" and Dagobert rose from his seat with a severe and painfully unquiet look.

"There now, Dagobert, you have begun to scold us already."

"Just at the very commencement," added Blanche.

"Commencement! - what, is there to be a sequel? a finish?"

"A finish? we hope not," said Rose, laughing like mad.

"All we ask is, that it should last forever," added Blanche, sharing in the hilarity of her sister.

Dagobert looked gravely from one to the other of the two maidens, as if trying to guess this enigma; but when he saw their sweet, innocent faces gracefully animated by a frank, ingenuous laugh, he reflected that they would not be so gay if they had any serious matter for self-reproach, and he felt pleased at seeing them so merry in the midst of their precarious position.

"Laugh on, my children!" he said. "I like so much to see you laugh."

Then, thinking that was not precisely the way in which he ought to treat the singular confession of the young girls, he added in a gruff voice: "Yes, I like to see you laugh - but not when you receive fair visitors with blue eyes, young ladies! - Come, acknowledge that I'm an old fool to listen to such nonsense - you are only making game of me."

"Nay, what we tell you is quite true."

"You know we never tell stories," added Rose.

"They are right - they never fib," said the soldier, in renewed perplexity.

"But how the devil is such a visit possible? I sleep before your door - Spoil-sport sleeps under your window - and all the blue eyes and fair locks in the world must come in by one of those two ways - and, if they had tried it, the dog and I, who have both of us quick ears, would have received their visits after our fashion. But come, children! pray, speak to the purpose. Explain yourselves!"

The two sisters, who saw, by the expression of Dagobert's countenance, that he felt really uneasy, determined no longer to trifle with his kindness. They exchanged a glance, and Rose, taking in her little hand the coarse, broad palm of the veteran, said to him: "Come, do not plague yourself! We will tell you all about the visits of our friend, Gabriel."

"There you are again! - He has a name, then?"

"Certainly, he has a name. It is Gabriel."

"Is it not a pretty name, Dagobert? Oh, you will see and love, as we do, our beautiful Gabriel!"

"I'll love your beautiful Gabriel, will I?" said the veteran, shaking his head - "Love your beautiful Gabriel? - that's as it may be. I must first know -" Then, interrupting himself, he added: "It is queer. That reminds me of something."

"Of what, Dagobert?"

"Fifteen years ago, in the last letter that your father, on his return from France, brought me from my wife: she told me that, poor as she was, and with our little growing Agricola on her hands, she had taken in a poor deserted child, with the face of a cherub, and the name of Gabriel - and only a short time since I heard of him again."

"And from whom, then?"

"You shall know that by and by."

"Well, then - since you have a Gabriel of your own - there is the more reason that you should love ours."

"Yours! but who is yours? I am on thorns till you tell me."

"You know, Dagobert," resumed Rose, "that Blanche and I are accustomed to fall asleep, holding each other by the hand."

"Yes, yes, I have often seen you in your cradle. I was never tired of looking at you; it was so pretty."

"Well, then - two nights ago, we had just fallen asleep, when we beheld -"

"Oh, it was in a dream!" cried Dagobert. "Since you were asleep, it was in a dream!"

"Certainly, in a dream - how else would you have it?"

"Pray let my sister go on with her tale!"

"All, well and good!" said the soldier with a sigh of satisfaction; "well and good! To be sure, I was tranquil enough in any case - because - but still - I like it better to be a dream. Continue, my little Rose."

"Once asleep, we both dreamt the same thing."

"What! both the same?"

"Yes, Dagobert; for the next morning when we awoke we related our two dreams to each other."

"And they were exactly alike."

"That's odd enough, my children; and what was this dream all about?"

"In our dream, Blanche and I were seated together, when we saw enter a beautiful angel, with a long white robe, fair locks, blue eyes, and so handsome and benign a countenance, that we elapsed our hands as if to pray to him. Then he told us, in a soft voice, that he was called Gabriel; that our mother had sent him to be our guardian angel, and that he would never abandon us."

"And, then," added Blanche, "he took us each by the hand, and, bending his fair face over us, looked at us for a long time in silence, with so much goodness - with so much goodness, that we could not withdraw our eyes from his."

"Yes," resumed Rose, "and his look seemed, by turns, to attract us, or to go to our hearts. At length, to our great sorrow, Gabriel quitted us, having told us that we should see him again the following night."

"And did he make his appearance?"

"Certainly. Judge with what impatience we waited the moment of sleep, to see if our friend would return, and visit us in our slumbers."

"Humph!" said Dagobert, scratching his forehead; "this reminds me, young ladies, that you kept on rubbing your eyes last evening, and pretending to be half asleep. I wager, it was all to send me away the sooner, and to get to your dream as fast as possible."

"Yes, Dagobert."

"The reason being, you could not say to me, as you would to Spoil-sport: Lie down, Dagobert! Well - so your friend Gabriel came back?"

"Yes, and this time he talked to us a great deal, and gave us, in the name of our mother, such touching, such noble counsels, that the next day, Rose and I spent our whole time in recalling every word of our guardian angel - and his face, and his look -"

"This reminds me again, young ladies, that you were whispering all along the road this morning; and that when I spoke of white, you answered black."

"Yes, Dagobert, we were thinking of Gabriel."

"And, ever since, we love him as well as he loves us."

"But he is only one between both of you!"

"Was not our mother one between us?"

"And you, Dagobert - are you not also one for us both?"

"True, true! And yet, do you know, I shall finish by being jealous of that Gabriel?"

"You are our friend by day - he is our friend by night."

"Let's understand it clearly. If you talk of him all day, and dream of him all night, what will there remain for me?"

"There will remain for you your two orphans, whom you love so much," said Rose.

"And who have only you left upon earth," added Blanche, in a caressing tongue.

"Humph! humph! that's right, coax the old man over, Nay, believe me, my children," added the soldier, tenderly, "I am quite satisfied with my lot. I can afford to let you have your Gabriel. I felt sure that Spoil sport and myself could take our rest in quiet. After all, there is nothing so astonishing in what you tell me; your first dream struck your fancy, and you talked so much about it that you had a second; nor should I be surprised if you were to see this fine fellow a third time."

"Oh, Dagobert! do not make a jest of it! They are only dreams, but we think our mother sends them to us. Did she not tell us that orphan children were watched over by guardian angels? Well, Gabriel is our guardian angel; he will protect us, and he will protect you also."

"Very kind of him to think of me; but you see, my dear children, for the matter of defence, I prefer the dog; he is less fair than your angel, but he has better teeth, and that is more to be depended on."

"How provoking you are, Dagobert - always jesting!"

"It is true; you can laugh at everything."

"Yes, I am astonishingly gay; I laugh with my teeth shut, in the style of old Jovial. Come, children, don't scold me: I know I am wrong. The remembrance of your dear mother is mixed with this dream, and you do well to speak of it seriously. Besides," added he, with a grave air, "dreams will sometimes come true. In Spain, two of the Empress's dragoons, comrades of mine, dreamt, the night before their death, that they would be poisoned by the monks - and so it happened. If you continue to dream of this fair angel Gabriel, it is - it is - why, it is, because you are amused by it; and, as you have none too many pleasures in the daytime, you may as well get an agreeable sleep at night. But, now, my children, I have also much to tell you; it will concern your mother; promise me not to be sad."

"Be satisfied! when we think of her we are not sad, though serious."

"That is well. For fear of grieving you, I have always delayed the moment of telling what your poor mother would have confided to you as soon as you were no longer children. But she died before she had time to do so, and that which I have to tell broke her heart - as it nearly did mine. I put off this communication as long as I could, taking for pretext that I would say nothing till we came to the field of battle where your father was made prisoner. That gave me time; but the moment is now come; I can shuffle it off no longer."

"We listen, Dagobert," responded the two maidens, with an attentive and melancholy air.

After a moment's silence, during which he appeared to reflect, the veteran thus addressed the young girls:

"Your father, General Simon, was the son of a workman, who remained a workman; for, notwithstanding all that the general could say or do, the old man was obstinate in not quitting his trade. He had a heart of gold and a head of iron, just like his son. You may suppose, my children, that when your father, who had enlisted as a private soldier, became a general and a count of the empire, it was not without toil or without glory."

"A count of the Empire! what is that, Dagobert?"

"Flummery - a title, which the Emperor gave over and above

the promotion, just for the sake of saying to the people, whom he loved because he was one of them: Here, children! You wish to play at nobility! You shall be nobles. You wish to play at royalty! You shall be kings. Take what you like - nothing is too good for you - enjoy yourselves!"

"Kings!" said the two girls, joining their hands in admiration.

"Kings of the first water. Oh, he was no niggard of his crowns, our Emperor! I had a bed-fellow of mine, a brave soldier, who was afterwards promoted to be king. This flattered us; for, if it was not one, it was the other. And so, at this game, your father became count; but, count or not, he was one of the best and bravest generals of the army."

"He was handsome, was he not, Dagobert? - mother always said so."

"Oh, yes! indeed he was - but quite another thing from your fair guardian angel. Picture to yourself a fine, dark man, who looked splendid in his full uniform, and could put fire into the soldiers' hearts. With him to lead, we would have charged up into Heaven itself - that is, if Heaven had, permitted it," added Dagobert, not wishing to wound in any way the religious beliefs of the orphans.

"And father was as good as he was brave, Dagobert."

"Good, my children? Yes, I should say so! - He could bend a horse-shoe in his hand as you would bend a card, and the day he was taken prisoner he had cut down the Prussian artillery-men on their very cannon. With strength and courage like that, how could he be otherwise than good? It is then about nineteen years ago, not far from this place - on the spot I showed you before we arrived at the village - that the general, dangerously wounded, fell from his horse. I was following him at the time, and ran to his assistance. Five minutes after we were made prisoners - and by whom think you? - by a Frenchman."

Eugene Sue

"A Frenchman?"

"Yes, an emigrant marquis, a colonel in the service of Russia," answered Dagobert, with bitterness. "And so, when this marquis advanced towards us, and said to the general: 'Surrender, sir, to a countryman!' - 'A Frenchman, who fights against France,' replied the general, 'is no longer my country-man; he is a traitor, and I'd never surrender to a traitor!' And, wounded though he was, he dragged himself up to a Russian grenadier, and delivered him his sabre, saying: 'I surrender to you my brave fellow!' The marquis became pale with rage at it."

The orphans looked at each other with pride, and a rich crimson mantled their cheeks, as they exclaimed: "Oh, our brave father!"

"Ah, those children," said Dagobert, as he proudly twirled his moustache. "One sees they have soldier's blood in their veins! Well," he continued, "we were now prisoners. The general's last horse had been killed under him; and, to perform the journey, he mounted Jovial, who had not been wounded that day. We arrived at Warsaw, and there it was that the general first saw your mother. She was called the Pearl of Warsaw; that is saying everything. Now he, who admired all that is good and beautiful, fell in love with her almost immediately; and she loved him in return; but her parents had promised her to another - and that other was the same -"

Dagobert was unable to proceed. Rose uttered a piercing cry, and pointed in terror to the window.

CHAPTER VII

THE TRAVELER

Upon the cry of the young girl, Dagobert rose abruptly.

"What is the matter, Rose?"

"There - there!" she said, pointing to the window. "I thought I saw a hand move the pelisse."

She had not concluded these words before Dagobert rushed to the window and opened it, tearing down the mantle, which had been suspended from the fastening.

It was still dark night, and the wind was blowing hard. The soldier listened, but could hear nothing.

Returning to fetch the lamp from the table, he shaded the flame with his hand, and strove to throw the light outside. Still he saw nothing. Persuaded that a gust of wind had disturbed and shaken the pelisse: and that Rose had been deceived by her own fears he again shut the window.

"Be satisfied, children! The wind is very high; it is that which lifted the corner of the pelisse."

"Yet methought I saw plainly the fingers which had hold of it," said Rose, still trembling.

Eugene Sue

"I was looking at Dagobert," said Blanche, "and I saw nothing."

"There was nothing to see, my children; the thing is clear enough. The window is at least eight feet above the ground; none but a giant could reach it without a ladder. Now, had any one used a ladder, there would not have been time to remove it; for, as soon as Rose cried out, I ran to the window, and, when I held out the light, I could see nothing."

"I must have been deceived," said Rose.

"You may be sure, sister, it was only the wind," added Blanche.

"Then I beg pardon for having disturbed you, my good Dagobert."

"Never mind!" replied the soldier musingly, "I am only sorry that Spoil sport is not come back. He would have watched the window, and that would have quite tranquillized you. But he no doubt scented the stable of his comrade, Jovial, and will have called in to bid him good-night on the road. I have half a mind to go and fetch him."

"Oh, no, Dagobert! do not leave us alone," cried the maidens; "we are too much afraid."

"Well, the dog is not likely to remain away much longer, and I am sure we shall soon hear him scratching at the door, so we will continue our story," said Dagobert, as he again seated himself near the head of the bed, but this time with his face towards the window.

"Now the general was prisoner at Warsaw," continued he, "and in love with your mother, whom they wished to marry to another. In 1814, we learned the finish of the war, the banishment of the Emperor to the Isle of Elba, and the return of the Bourbons. In concert with the Prussians and Russians, who had brought them back, they had exiled the Emperor.

Learning all this, your mother said to the general: 'The war is finished; you are free, but your Emperor is in trouble. You owe everything to him; go and join him in his misfortunes. I know not when we shall meet again, but I shall never marry any one but you, I am yours till death!' – Before he set out the general called me to him, and said: 'Dagobert, remain here; Mademoiselle Eva may have need of you to fly from her family, if they should press too hard upon her; our correspondence will have to pass through your hands; at Paris, I shall see your wife and son; I will comfort them, and tell them you are my friend.'"

"Always the same," said Rose, with emotion, as she looked affectionately at Dagobert.

"As faithful to the father and mother as to their children," added Blanche.

"To love one was to love them all," replied the soldier. "Well, the general joined the Emperor at Elba; I remained at Warsaw, concealed in the neighborhood of your mother's house; I received the letters, and conveyed them to her clandestinely. In one of those letters - I feel proud to tell you of it my children - the general informed me that the Emperor himself had remembered me."

"What, did he know you?"

"A little, I flatter myself - 'Oh! Dagobert!' said he to your father, who was talking to him about me; 'a horse-grenadier of my old guard - a soldier of Egypt and Italy, battered with wounds - an old dare-devil, whom I decorated with my own hand at Wagram - I have not forgotten him!' - I vow, children, when your mother read that to me, I cried like a fool."

"The Emperor - what a fine golden face he has on the silver cross with the red ribbon that you would sometimes show us when we behaved well."

"That cross - given by him - is my relic. It is there in my

knapsack, with whatever we have of value - our little purse and papers. But, to return to your mother; it was a great consolation to her, when I took her letters from the general, or talked with her about him - for she suffered much - oh, so much! In vain her parents tormented and persecuted her; she always answered: 'I will never marry any one but General Simon.' A spirited woman, I can tell you - resigned, but wonderfully courageous. One day she received a letter from the general; he had left the Isle of Elba with the Emperor; the war had again broken out, a short campaign, but as fierce as ever, and heightened by soldiers' devotion. In that campaign of France; my children, especially at Montmirail, your father fought like a lion, and his division followed his example it was no longer valor - it was frenzy. He told me that, in Champagne, the peasants killed so many of those Prussians, that their fields were manured with them for years. Men, women, children, all rushed upon them. Pitchforks, stones, mattocks, all served for the slaughter. It was a true wolf hunt!"

The veins swelled on the soldier's forehead, and his cheeks flushed as he spoke, for this popular heroism recalled to his memory the sublime enthusiasm of the wars of the republic - those armed risings of a whole people, from which dated the first steps of his military career, as the triumphs of the Empire were the last days of his service.

The orphans, too, daughters of a soldier and a brave woman, did not shrink from the rough energy of these words, but felt their cheeks glow, and their hearts beat tumultuously.

"How happy we are to be the children of so brave a father!" cried Blanche.

"It is a happiness and an honor too, my children - for the evening of the battle of Montmirail, the Emperor, to the joy of the whole army, made your father Duke of Ligny and Marshal of France."

"Marshal of France!" said Rose in astonishment, without

understanding the exact meaning of the words.

"Duke of Ligny!" added Blanche with equal surprise.

"Yes; Peter Simon, the son of a workman, became duke and marshal - there is nothing higher except a king!" resumed Dagobert, proudly. "That's how the Emperor treated the sons of the people, and, therefore, the people were devoted to him. It was all very fine to tell them 'Your Emperor makes you food for cannon.' 'Stuff!' replied the people, who are no fools, 'another would make us food for misery. We prefer the cannon, with the chance of becoming captain or colonel, marshal, king - or invalid; that's better than to perish with hunger, cold, and age, on straw in a garret, after toiling forty years for others.'"

"Even in France - even in Paris, that beautiful city - do you mean to say there are poor people who die of hunger and misery, Dagobert?"

"Even in Paris? Yes, my children; therefore, I come back to the point, the cannon is better. With it, one has the chance of becoming, like your father, duke and marshal: when I say duke and marshal, I am partly right and partly wrong, for the title and the rank were not recognized in the end; because, after Montmirail, came a day of gloom, a day of great mourning, when, as the general has told me, old soldiers like myself wept - yes, wept! - on the evening of a battle. That day, my children, was Waterloo!"

There was in these simple words of Dagobert an expression of such deep sorrow, that it thrilled the hearts of the orphans.

"Alas!" resumed the soldier, with a sigh, "there are days which seem to have a curse on them. That same day, at Waterloo, the general fell, covered with wounds, at the head of a division of the Guards. When he was nearly cured, which was not for a long time, he solicited permission to go to St. Helena - another island at the far end of the world, to which the English had

Eugene Sue

carried the Emperor, to torture him at their leisure; for if he was very fortunate in the first instance, he had to go through a deal of hard rubs at last, my poor children."

"If you talk in that way, you will make us cry, Dagobert."

"There is cause enough for it - the Emperor suffered so much! He bled cruelly at the heart believe me. Unfortunately, the general was not with him at St. Helena; he would have been one more to console him; but they would not allow him to go. Then, exasperated, like so many others, against the Bourbons, the general engaged in a conspiracy to recall the son of the Emperor. He relied especially on one regiment, nearly all composed of his old soldiers, and he went down to a place in Picardy, where they were then in garrison; but the conspiracy had already been divulged. Arrested the moment of his arrival, the general was taken before the colonel of the regiment. And this colonel," said the soldier, after a brief pause, "who do you think it was again? Bah! it would be too long to tell you all, and would only make you more sad; but it was a man whom your father had many reasons to hate. When he found himself face to face with him, he said: 'if you are not a coward, you will give me one hour's liberty, and we will fight to the death; I hate you for this, I despise you for that' - and so on. The colonel accepted the challenge, and gave your father his liberty till the morrow. The duel was a desperate one; the colonel was left for dead on the spot."

"Merciful heaven!"

"The general was yet wiping his sword, when a faithful friend came to him, and told him he had only just time to save himself. In fact, he happily succeeded in leaving France - yes, happily - for a fortnight after, he was condemned to death as a conspirator."

"What misfortunes, good heaven!"

"There was some luck, however, in the midst of his troubles.

Your mother had kept her promise bravely, and was still waiting for him. She had written to him: 'The Emperor first, and me next!' both unable to do anything more for the Emperor, nor even for his son, the general, banished from France, set out for Warsaw. Your mother had lost her parents, and was now free; they were married - and I am one of the witnesses to the marriage."

"You are right, Dagobert; that was great happiness in the midst of great misfortunes!"

"Yes, they were very happy; but, as it happened with all good hearts, the happier they were themselves, the more they felt for the sorrows of others - and there was quite enough to grieve them at Warsaw. The Russians had again begun to treat the Poles as their slaves; your brave mother, though of French origin, was a Pole in heart and soul; she spoke out boldly what others did not dare speak in a whisper, and all the unfortunate called her their protecting angel. That was enough to excite the suspicions of the Russian governor. One day, a friend of the general's, formerly a colonel in the lancers, a brave and worthy man, was condemned to be exiled to Siberia for a military plot against the Russians. He took refuge in your father's house, and lay hid there; but his retreat was discovered. During the next night, a party of Cossacks, commanded by an officer, and followed by a travelling-carriage, arrive at our door; they rouse the general from his sleep and take him away with them."

"Oh, heaven! what did they mean to do with him?"

"Conduct him out of the Russian dominions, with a charge never to return, on pain of perpetual imprisonment. His last words were: 'Dagobert, I entrust to thee my wife and child!' - for it wanted yet some months of the time when you were to be born. Well, notwithstanding that, they exiled your mother to Siberia; it was an opportunity to get rid of her; she did too much good at Warsaw, and they feared her accordingly. Not content with banishing her, they confiscated all her property; the only favor she could obtain was, that I should accompany her, and, had it not been for Jovial, whom the general had given to me, she would have had to make the journey on foot. It was thus, with her on horseback, and I leading her as I lead you, my children, that we arrived at the poverty-stricken village, where, three months after, you poor little things were born!"

"And our father?"

"It was impossible for him to return to Russia; impossible for your mother to think of flight, with two children; impossible for the general to write to her, as he knew not where she was."

"So, since that time, you have had no news of him?"

"Yes, my children - once we had news."

"And by whom?"

After a moment's silence, Dagobert resumed with a singular expression of countenance: "By whom? - by one who is not like other men. Yes - that you may understand me better, I will relate to you an extraordinary adventure, which happened to your father during his last French campaign. He had been ordered by the Emperor to carry a battery, which was playing heavily on our army; after several unsuccessful efforts, the general put himself at the head of a regiment of cuirassiers, and charged the battery, intending, as was his custom, to cut down the men at their guns. He was on horseback, just before the mouth of a cannon, where all the artillerymen had been either killed or wounded, when one of them still found strength to raise himself upon one knee, and to apply the lighted match to the touchhole - and that when your father was about ten paces in front of the loaded piece."

"Oh! what a peril for our father!"

"Never, he told me, had he run such imminent danger for he saw the artilleryman apply the match, and the gun go off - but, at the very nick, a man of tall stature, dressed as a peasant, and whom he had not before remarked, threw himself in front of the cannon."

"Unfortunate creature! what a horrible death!"

"Yes," said Dagobert, thoughtfully; "it should have been so. He ought by rights to have been blown into a thousand pieces. But no - nothing of the kind!"

"What do you tell us?"

"What the general told me. 'At the moment when the gun went off,' as he often repeated to me, 'I shut my eyes by an involuntary movement, that I might not see the mutilated body of the poor wretch who had sacrificed himself in my place. When I again opened them, the first thing I saw in the midst of the smoke, was the tall figure of this man, standing erect and calm on the same spot, and casting a sad mild look on the artilleryman, who, with one knee on the ground, and his body thrown backward, gazed on him in as much terror as if he had been the devil. Afterwards, I lost sight of this man in the tumult,' added your father."

"Bless me Dagobert! how can this be possible?"

"That is just what I said to the general. He answered me that he had never been able to explain to himself this event, which seemed as incredible as it was true. Moreover, your father must have been greatly struck with the countenance of this man, who appeared, he said, about thirty years of age - for he remarked, that his extremely black eyebrows were joined together, and formed, as it were, one line from temple to temple, so that he seemed to have a black streak across his forehead. Remember this, my children; you will soon see why."

"Oh, Dagobert! we shall not forget it," said the orphans, growing more and more astonished as he proceeded.

Eugene Sue

"Is it not strange - this man with a black seam on his forehead?"

"Well, you shall hear. The general had, as I told you, been left for dead at Waterloo. During the night which he passed on the field of battle, in a sort of delirium brought on by the fever of his wounds, he saw, or fancied he saw, this same man bending over him, with a look of great mildness and deep melancholy, stanching his wounds, and using every effort to revive him. But as your father, whose senses were still wandering, repulsed his kindness saying, that after such a defeat, it only remained to die - it appeared as if this man replied to him; 'You must live for Eva!' meaning your mother, whom the general had left at Warsaw, to join the Emperor, and make this campaign of France."

"How strange, Dagobert! - And since then, did our father never see this man?"

"Yes, he saw him - for it was he who brought news of the general to your poor mother."

"When was that? We never heard of it."

"You remember that, on the day your mother died, you went to the pine forest with old Fedora?"

"Yes," answered Rose, mournfully; "to fetch some heath, of which our mother was so fond."

"Poor mother!" added Blanche; "she appeared so well that morning, that we could not dream of the calamity which awaited us before night."

"True, my children; I sang and worked that morning in the garden, expecting, no more than you did, what was to happen. Well, as I was singing at my work, on a sudden I heard a voice ask me in French: 'Is this the village of Milosk?' - I turned round, and saw before me a stranger; I looked at him attentively, and, instead of replying, fell back two steps, quite stupefied."

"Ah, why?"

"He was of tall stature, very pale, with a high and open forehead; but his eyebrows met, and seemed to form one black streak across it."

"Then it was the same man who had twice been with our father in battle?"

"Yes - it was he."

"But, Dagobert," said Rose, thoughtfully, "is it not a long time since these battles?"

"About sixteen years."

"And of what age was this stranger?"

"Hardly more than thirty."

"Then how can it be the same man, who sixteen years before, had been with our father in the wars?"

"You are right," said Dagobert, after a moment's silence, and shrugging his shoulders: "I may have been deceived by a chance likeness - and yet -"

"Or, if it were the same, he could not have got older all that while."

"But did you ask him, if he had not formerly relieved our father?"

"At first I was so surprised that I did not think of it; and afterwards, he remained so short a time, that I had no opportunity. Well, he asked me for the village of Milosk. 'You are there, sir,' said I, 'but how do you know that I am a Frenchman?' 'I heard you singing as I passed,' replied he; 'could you tell me the house of Madame Simon, the general's wife?' 'She lives here, sir.' Then looking at me for some seconds in silence, he took me by the hand and said: 'You are the friend of General Simon - his best friend?' Judge of my astonishment, as I answered: 'But, sir, how do you know?' 'He has often spoken of you with gratitude.' 'You have seen the general then?' 'Yes, some time ago, in India. I am also his friend: I bring news of him to his wife, whom I knew to be exiled in Siberia. At Tobolsk, whence I come, I learned that she inhabits this village. Conduct me to her!'"

"The good traveller - I love him already," said Rose.

"Yes, being father's friend."

"I begged him to wait an instant, whilst I went to inform your mother, so that the surprise might not do her harm; five minutes after, he was beside her."

"And what kind of man was this traveller, Dagobert?"

"He was very tall; he wore a dark pelisse, and a fur cap, and had long black hair."

"Was he handsome?"

"Yes, my children - very handsome; but with so mild and melancholy an air, that it pained my heart to see him."

"Poor man! he had doubtless known some great sorrow."

"Your mother had been closeted with him for some minutes, when she called me to her and said that she had just received good news of the general. She was in tears, and had before her a large packet of papers; it was a kind of journal, which your father had written every evening to console himself; not being able to speak to her, he told the paper all that he would have told her."

"Oh! where are these papers, Dagobert?"

"There, in the knapsack, with my cross and our purse. One day I will give them to you: but I have picked out a few leaves here and there for you to read presently. You will see why."

"Had our father been long in India?"

"I gathered from the few words which your mother said, that the general had gone to that country, after fighting for the Greeks against the Turks - for he always liked to side with the weak against the strong. In India he made fierce war against the English, they had murdered our prisoners in pontoons, and tortured the Emperor at St. Helena, and the war was a doubly good one, for in harming them he served a just cause."

"What cause did he serve then?"

"That of one of the poor native princes, whose territories the English, lay waste, till the day when they can take possession of them against law and right. You see, my children, it was once more the weak against the strong, and your father did not miss this opportunity. In a few months he had so well-trained and disciplined the twelve or fifteen thousand men of the prince, that, in two encounters, they cut to pieces the English sent against them, and who, no doubt, had in their reckoning left out your brave father, my children. But come, you shall read some pages of his journal, which will tell you more and better than I can. Moreover, you will find in them a name which you ought always to remember; that's why I chose this passage."

"Oh, what happiness! To read the pages written by our father, is almost to hear him speak," said Rose.

"It is as if he were close beside us," added Blanche.

And the girls stretched out their hands with eagerness, to catch hold of the leaves that Dagobert had taken from his pocket. Then, by a simultaneous movement, full of touching grace, they pressed the writing of their father in silence to their lips.

"You will see also, my children, at the end of this letter, why I was surprised that your guardian angel, as you say, should be called Gabriel. Read, read," added the soldier, observing the puzzled air of the orphans. "Only I ought to tell you that, when he wrote this, the general had not yet fallen in with the traveller who brought the papers."

Rose, sitting up in her bed, took the leaves, and began to read in a soft and trembling voice, Blanche, with her head resting on her sister's shoulder, followed attentively every word. One could even see, by the slight motion of her lips, that she too was reading, but only to herself.

CHAPTER VIII

EXTRACTS FROM GENERAL SIMON'S DIARY

Bivouac on the Mountains of Avers February the 20th, 1830.

"Each time I add some pages to this journal, written now in the heart of India, where the fortune of my wandering and proscribed existence has thrown me - a journal which, alas! my beloved Eva, you may never read - I experience a sweet, yet painful emotion; for, although to converse thus with you is a consolation, it brings back the bitter thought that I am unable to see or speak to you.

"Still, if these pages should ever meet your eyes, your generous heart will throb at the name of the intrepid being, to whom I am this day indebted for my life, and to whom I may thus perhaps owe the happiness of seeing you again - you and my child - for of course our child lives. Yes, it must be - for else, poor wife, what an existence would be yours amid the horrors of exile! Dear soul! he must now be fourteen. Whom does he resemble? Is he like you? Has he your large and beautiful blue eyes? - Madman that I am! how many times, in this long day-book, have I already asked the same idle question, to which you can return no answer! - How many times shall I continue to ask it? - But you will teach our child to speak and love the somewhat savage name of Djalma."

"Djalma!" said Rose, as with moist eyes she left off reading.

Eugene Sue

"Djalma!" repeated Blanche, who shared the emotion of her sister. "Oh, we shall never forget that name."

"And you will do well, my children; for it seems to be the name of a famous soldier, though a very young one. But go on, my little Rose!"

"I have told you in the preceding pages, my dear Eva, of the two glorious days we had this month. The troops of my old friend, the prince, which daily make fresh advances in European discipline, have performed wonders. We have beaten the English, and obliged them to abandon a portion of this unhappy country, which they had invaded in contempt of all the rights of justice, and which they continue to ravage without mercy, for, in these parts, warfare is another name for treachery, pillage, and massacre. This morning, after a toilsome march through a rocky and mountainous district, we received information from our scouts, that the enemy had been reinforced, and was preparing to act on the offensive; and, as we were separated from them by a distance of a few leagues only, an engagement became inevitable. My old friend the prince, the father of my deliverer, was impatient to march to the attack. The action began about three o'clock; it was very bloody and furious. Seeing that our men wavered for a moment, for they were inferior in number, and the English reinforcements consisted of fresh troops, I charged at the head of our weak reserve of cavalry. The old prince was in the centre, fighting, as he always fights, intrepidly; his son, Djalma, scarcely eighteen, as brave as his father, did not leave my side. In the hottest part of the engagement, my horse was killed under me, and rolling over into a ravine, along the edge of which I was riding, I found myself so awkwardly entangled beneath him, that for an instant I thought my thigh was broken."

"Poor father!" said Blanche.

"This time, happily, nothing more dangerous ensued thanks to Djalma! You see, Dagobert," added Rose, "that I remember the name." And she continued to read,

"The English thought - and a very flattering opinion it was - that, if they could kill me, they would make short work of the prince's army. So a Sepoy officer, with five or six irregulars - cowardly, ferocious plunderers - seeing me roll down the ravine, threw themselves into it to despatch me. Surrounded by fire and smoke, and carried away by their ardor, our mountaineers had not seen me fall; but Djalma never left me. He leaped into the ravine to my assistance, and his cool intrepidity saved my life. He had held the fire of his double-barrelled carbine; with one load, he killed the officer on the spot; with the other he broke the arm of an irregular, who had already pierced my left hand with his bayonet. But do not be alarmed, dear Eva; it is nothing - only a scratch."

"Wounded - again wounded - alas!" cried Blanche, clasping her hands together, and interrupting her sister.

"Take courage!" said Dagobert: "I dare say it was only a scratch, as the general calls it. Formerly, he used to call wounds, which did not disable a man from fighting, blank wounds. There was no one like him for such sayings."

"Djalma, seeing me wounded," resumed Rose, wiping her eyes, "made use of his heavy carbine as a club, and drove back the soldiers. At that instant, I perceived a new assailant, who, sheltered behind a clump of bamboos which commanded the ravine, slowly lowered his long gun, placed the barrel between two branches, and took deliberate aim at Djalma. Before my shouts could apprise him of his danger, the brave youth had received a ball in his breast. Feeling himself hit, he fell bark involuntarily two paces, and dropped upon one knee: but he still remained firm, endeavoring to cover me with his body. You may conceive my rage and despair, whilst all my efforts to disengage myself were paralyzed by the excruciating pain in my thigh. Powerless and disarmed, I witnessed for some moments this unequal struggle.

Eugene Sue

"Djalma was losing blood rapidly; his strength of arm began to fail him; already one of the irregulars, inciting his comrades with his voice, drew from his belt a huge, heavy kind of billhook, when a dozen of our mountaineers made their appearance, borne towards the spot by the irresistible current of the battle. Djalma was rescued in his turn, I was released, and, in a quarter of an hour, I was able to mount a horse. The fortune of the day is ours, though with severe loss; but the fires of the English camp are still visible, and to-morrow the conflict will be decisive. Thus, my beloved Eva, I owe my life to this youth. Happily, his wound occasions us no uneasiness; the ball only glanced along the ribs in a slanting direction."

"The brave boy might have said: 'A blank wound,' like the general," observed Dagobert.

"Now, my dear Eva," continued Rose, "you must become acquainted, by means of this narrative at least, with the intrepid Djalma. He is but just eighteen. With one word, I will paint for you his noble and valiant nature; it is a custom of this country to give surnames, and, when only fifteen, he was called 'The Generous' - by which was, of course, meant generous in heart and mind. By another custom, no less touching than whimsical, this name was reverted to his parent, who is called 'The Father of the Generous,' and who might, with equal propriety, be called 'The Just,' for this old Indian is a rare example of chivalrous honor and proud independence. He might, like so many other poor princes of this country, have humbled himself before the execrable despotism of the English, bargained for the relinquishment of sovereign power, and submitted to brute force - but it was not in his nature. 'My whole rights, or a grave in my native mountains!' - such is his motto. And this is no empty boast; it springs from the conviction of what is right and just. 'But you will be crushed in the struggle,' I have said to him - 'My friend,' he answered, 'what if, to force you to a disgraceful act, you were told to yield or die?' - From that day I understood him, and have devoted myself, mind and body, to the ever sacred cause of the weak against the strong. You see, my Eva, that Djalma shows himself worthy of such a father. This young Indian is so proud, so heroic in his bravery, that, like a young Greek of Leonidas' age, he fights with his breast bare; while other warriors of his country (who, indeed, usually have arms, breast, and shoulders uncovered) wear, in time of battle, a thick, impenetrable vest. The rash daring of this youth reminds me of Murat, King of Naples, who, I have so often told you, I have seen a hundred times leading the most desperate charges with nothing but a riding-whip in his hand."

"That's another of those kings I was telling you of, whom the Emperor set up for his amusement," said Dagobert. "I once saw a Prussian officer prisoner, whose face had been cut across by that mad-cap King of Naples' riding-whip; the mark was there, a black and blue stripe. The Prussian swore he was dishonored, and that a sabre-cut would have been preferable. I should rather think so! That devil of a king; he only had one idea: 'Forward, on to the cannon!' As soon as they began to cannonade, one would have thought the guns were calling him with all their might, for he was soon up to them with his 'Here I am!' If I speak to you about him, my children, it's because he was fond of repeating, - 'No one can break through a square of infantry, if General Simon or I can't do it.'"

Rose continued:

"I have observed with pain, that, notwithstanding his youth, Djalma is often subject to fits of deep melancholy. At times, I have seen him exchange with his father looks of singular import. In spite of our mutual attachment, I believe that both conceal from me some sad family secret, in so far as I can judge from expressions which have dropped from them by chance.

"It relates to some strange event which their vivid imaginations have invested with a supernatural character.

"And yet, my love, you and I have no longer the right to smile at the credulity of others. I, since the French campaign, when I met with that extraordinary adventure, which, to this day, I am

Eugene Sue

quite unable to understand -"

"This refers to the man who threw himself before the mouth of the cannon," said Dagobert.

"And you," continued the maiden, still reading, "you, my dear Eva, since the visits of that young and beautiful woman, whom, as your mother asserted, she had seen at her mother's house forty years before."

The orphans, in amazement, looked at the soldier.

"Your mother never spoke to me of that, nor the general either, my children; this is as strange to me as it is to you."

With increasing excitement and curiosity, Rose continued:

"After all, my dear Eva, things which appear very extraordinary, may often be explained by a chance resemblance or a freak of nature. Marvels being always the result of optical illusion or heated fancy, a time must come, when that which appeared to be superhuman or supernatural, will prove to be the most simple and natural event in the world. I doubt not, therefore, that the things, which we denominate our prodigies, will one day receive this commonplace solution."

"You see, my children - things appear marvelous, which at bottom are quite simple - though for a long time we understand nothing about them."

"As our father relates this, we must believe it, and not be astonished - eh, sister?"

"Yes, truly - since it will all be explained one day."

"For example," said Dagobert, after a moment's reflection, "you two are so much alike, that any one, who was not in the habit of seeing you daily, might easily take one for the other. Well! if they did not know that you are, so to speak,'doubles,' they might think an imp was at work instead of such good little angels as you are."

"You are right, Dagobert; in this way many things may be explained, even as our father says." And Rose continued to read:

"Not without pride, my gentle Eva, have I learned that Djalma has French blood in his veins. His father married, some years ago, a young girl, whose family, of French origin, had long been settled at Batavia in the island of Java. This similarity of circumstances between my old friend and myself - for your family also, my Eva, is of French origin, and long settled in a foreign land - has only served to augment my sympathy for him. Unfortunately, he has long had to mourn the loss of the wife whom he adored.

"See, my beloved Eva! my hand trembles as I write these words. I am weak - I am foolish - but, alas! my heart sinks within me. If such a misfortune were to happen to me - Oh, my God! - what would become of our child without thee - without his father - in that barbarous country? But no! the very fear is madness; and yet what a horrible torture is uncertainty! Where may you now be? What are you doing? What has become of you? Pardon these black thoughts, which are sometimes too much for me. They are the cause of my worst moments - for, when free from them, I can at least say to myself: I am proscribed, I am every way unfortunate - but, at the other end of the world, two hearts still beat for me with affection - yours, my Eva, and our child's!"

Rose could hardly finish this passage; for some seconds her voice was broken by sobs. There was indeed a fatal coincidence between the fears of General Simon and the sad reality; and what could be more touching than these outpourings of the heart, written by the light of a watch fire, on the eve of battle, by a soldier who thus sought to soothe the pangs of a separation, which he felt bitterly, but knew not would be eternal?

"Poor general! he is unaware of our misfortune," said Dagobert, after a moment's silence; "but neither has he heard that he has two children, instead of one. That will be at least some consolation. But come, Blanche; do go on reading: I fear that this dwelling on grief fatigues your sister, and she is too much affected by it. Besides, after all, it is only just, that you should take your share of its pleasure and its sorrow."

Blanche took the letter, and Rose, having dried her eyes, laid in her turn her sweet head on the shoulder of her sister, who thus continued:

"I am calmer now, my dear Eva; I left off writing for a moment, and strove to banish those black presentiments. Let us resume our conversation! After discoursing so long about India, I will talk to you a little of Europe. Yesterday evening, one of our people (a trusty fellow) rejoined our outposts. He brought me a letter, which had arrived from France at Calcutta; at length, I have news of my father, and am no longer anxious on his account. This letter is dated in August of last year. I see by its contents, that several other letters, to which he alludes, have either been delayed or lost; for I had not received any for two years before, and was extremely uneasy about him. But my excellent father is the same as ever! Age has not weakened him; his character is as energetic, his health as robust, as in times past - still a workman, still proud of his order, still faithful to his austere republican ideas, still hoping much.

"For he says to me, 'the time is at hand,' and he underlines those words. He gives me also, as you will see, good news of the family of old Dagobert, our friend - for in truth, my dear Eva, it soothes my grief to think, that this excellent man is with you, that he will have accompanied you in your exile - for I know him - a kernel of gold beneath the rude rind of a soldier! How he must love our child!"

Here Dagobert coughed two or three times, stooped down, and appeared to be seeking on the ground the little red and blue check-handkerchief spread over his knees. He remained thus bent for some seconds, and, when he raised himself, he drew his hand across his moustache.

"How well father knows you!"

"How rightly has he guessed that you would love us!"

"Well, well, children; pass over that! - Let's come to the part where the general speaks of my little Agricola, and of Gabriel, my wife's adopted child. Poor woman! when I think that in three months perhaps - but come, child, read, read," added the old soldier, wishing to conceal his emotion.

"I still hope against hope, my dear Eva, that these pages will one day reach you, and therefore I wish to insert in them all that can be interesting to Dagobert. It will be a consolation to him, to have some news of his family. My father, who is still foreman at Mr. Hardy's, tells me that worthy man has also taken into his house the son of old Dagobert. Agricola works under my father, who is enchanted with him. He is, he tells me, a tall and vigorous lad, who wields the heavy forge hammer as if it were a feather, and is light-spirited as he is intelligent and laborious. He is the best workman on the establishment; and this does not prevent him in the evening, after his hard day's work, when he returns home to his mother, whom he truly loves, from making songs and writing excellent patriotic verses. His poetry is full of fire and energy; his fellow-workmen sing nothing else, and his lays have the power to warm the coldest and the most timid hearts."

"How proud you must be of your son, Dagobert," said Rose, in admiration; "he writes songs."

"Certainly, it is all very fine - but what pleases me best is, that he is good to his mother, and that he handles the hammer with a will. As for the songs, before he makes a 'Rising of the People,' or a 'Marseillaise,' he will have had to beat a good deal of iron; but where can this rascally sweet Agricola have learned to make songs at all? - No doubt, it was at school, where he went, as you will see, with his adopted brother Gabriel."

At this name of Gabriel, which reminded them of the imaginary being whom they called their guardian angel, the curiosity of the young girls was greatly excited. With redoubled attention, Blanche continued in these words:

"The adopted brother of Agricola, the poor deserted child whom the wife of our good Dagobert so generously took in, forms, my father tells me, a great contrast with Agricola; not in heart, for they have both excellent hearts; but Gabriel is as thoughtful and melancholy as Agricola is lively, joyous, and active. Moreover, adds my father, each of them, so to speak, has the aspect, which belongs to his character. Agricola is dark, tall, and strong, with a gay and bold air; Gabriel, on the contrary, is weak, fair, timid as a girl, and his face wears an expression of angelic mildness."

The orphans looked at each other in surprise; then, as they turned towards the soldier their ingenuous countenances, Rose said to him; "Have you heard, Dagobert? Father says, that your Gabriel is fair, and has the face of an angel. Why, 'tis exactly like ours!"

"Yes, yes, I heard very well; it is that which surprised me, in your dream."

"I should like to know, if he has also blue eyes," said Rose.

"As for that, my children, though the general says nothing about it, I will answer for it: your fair boys have always blue eyes. But, blue or black, he will not use them to stare at young ladies; go on, and you will see why."

Blanche resumed:

"His face wears an expression of angelic mildness. One of the Brothers of the Christian Schools, where he went with Agricola and other children of his quarter, struck with his intelligence and good disposition, spoke of him to a person of consequence, who, becoming interested in the lad, placed him in a seminary for the clergy, and, since the last two years, Gabriel is a priest. He intends devoting himself to foreign missions, and will soon set out for America."

"Your Gabriel is a priest, it appears?" said Rose, looking at Dagobert.

"While ours is an angel," added Blanche.

"Which only proves that yours is a step higher than mine. Well, every one to his taste; there are good people in all trades; but I prefer that it should be Gabriel who has chosen the black gown. I'd rather see my boy with arms bare, hammer in hand, and a leathern apron round him, neither more nor less than your old grandfather, my children - the father of Marshal Simon, Duke of Ligny - for, after all, marshal and duke he is by the grace of the Emperor. Now finish your letter."

"Soon, alas, yes!" said Blanche; "there are only a few lines left." And she proceeded:

"Thus, my dear, loving Eva, if this journal should ever reach its destination, you will be able to satisfy Dagobert as to the position of his wife and son, whom he left for our sakes. How can we ever repay such a sacrifice? But I feel sure, that your good and generous heart will have found some means of compensation.

"Adieu! - Again adieu, for to-day, my beloved Eva; I left off writing for a moment, to visit the tent of Djalma. He slept peacefully, and his father watched beside him; with a smile, he banished my fears. This intrepid young man is no longer in any danger. May he still be spared in the combat of to-morrow! Adieu, my gentle Eva! the night is silent and calm; the fires of the bivouac are slowly dying out, and our poor mountaineers repose after this bloody day; I can hear, from hour to hour, the distant all's well of our sentinels. Those foreign words bring back my grief; they remind me of what I sometimes forget in writing - that I am faraway, separated from you and from my child! Poor, beloved beings! what will be your destiny? Ah! if I could only send you, in time, that medal, which, by a fatal accident, I carried away with me from Warsaw, you might, perhaps, obtain leave to visit France, or at least to send our child there with Dagobert; for you know of what importance - But why add this sorrow to all the rest? Unfortunately, the years are passing away, the fatal day will arrive, and this last hope, in which I live for you, will also be taken from me: but I will not close the evening by so sad a thought. Adieu, my beloved Eva! Clasp our child to your bosom, and cover it with all the kisses which I send to both of you from the depths of exile!"

"Till to-morrow - after the battle!"

The reading of this touching letter was followed by long silence. The tears of Rose and Blanche flowed together. Dagobert, with his head resting on his hand, was absorbed in painful reflections.

Without doors, the wind had now augmented in violence; a heavy rain began to beat on the sounding panes; the most profound silence reigned in the interior of the inn. But, whilst the daughters of General Simon were reading with such deep emotion, these fragments of their father's journal, a strange and mysterious scene transpired in the menagerie of the brute-tamer.

CHAPTER IX

THE CAGES

Morok had prepared himself. Over his deer-skin vest he had drawn the coat of mail - that steel tissue, as pliable as cloth, as hard as diamonds; next, clothing his arms and legs in their proper armor, and his feet in iron-bound buskins, and concealing all this defensive equipment under loose trousers and an ample pelisse carefully buttoned, he took in his hand a long bar of iron, white-hot, set in a wooden handle.

Though long ago daunted by the skill and energy of the Prophet, his tiger Cain, his lion Judas, and his black panther Death, had sometimes attempted, in a moment of rebellion, to try their fangs and claws on his person; but, thanks to the armor concealed beneath his pelisse, they blunted their claws upon a skin of steel, and notched their fangs upon arms or legs of iron, whilst a slight touch of their master's metallic wand left a deep furrow in their smoking, shrivelled flesh.

Finding the inutility of their efforts, and endowed with strong memory, the beasts soon learned that their teeth and claws were powerless when directed against this invulnerable being. Hence, their terrified submission reached to such a point that, in his public representations, their master could make them crouch and cower at his feet by the least movement of a little wand covered with flame-colored paper.

The Prophet, thus armed with care, and holding in his hand

Eugene Sue

the iron made hot by Goliath, descended by the trapdoor of the loft into the large shed beneath, in which were deposited the cages of his animals. A mere wooden partition separated this shed from the stable that contained his horses.

A lantern, with a reflector, threw a vivid light on the cages. They were four in number. A wide iron grating formed their sides, turning at one end upon hinges like a door, so as to give ingress to the animal; the bottom of each den rested on two axle-trees and four small iron castors, so that they could easily be removed to the large covered wagon in which they were placed during a journey. One of them was empty; the other three contained, as already intimated, a panther, a tiger, and a lion.

The panther, originally from Java, seemed to merit the gloomy name of Death, by her grim, ferocious aspect. Completely black, she lay crouching and rolled up in the bottom of her cage, and her dark hues mingling with the obscurity which surrounded her, nothing was distinctly visible but fixed and glaring eyes - yellow balls of phosphoric light, which only kindled, as it were, in the night-time; for it is the nature of all the animals of the feline species to enjoy entire clearness of vision but in darkness.

The Prophet entered the stable in silence: the dark red of his long pelisse contrasted with the pale yellow of his straight hair and beard; the lantern, placed at some height above the ground, threw its rays full upon this man, and the strong light, opposed to the deep shadows around it, gave effect to the sharp proportions of his bony and savage looking figure.

He approached the cage slowly. The white rim, which encircled his eyeball, appeared to dilate, and his look rivaled in motionless brilliancy the steadily sparkling gaze of the panther. Still crouching in the shade, she felt already the fascination of that glance; two or three times she dropped her eyelids, with a low, angry howl; then, reopening her eyes, as if in spite of herself, she kept them fastened immovably on those of the

Prophet. And now her rounded ears clung to her skull, which was flattened like a viper's; the skin of her forehead became convulsively wrinkled; she drew in her bristling, but silky muzzle, and twice silently opened her jaws, garnished with formidable fangs. From that moment a kind of magnetic connection seemed to be established between the man and the beast.

The Prophet extended his glowing bar towards the cage, and said, in a sharp, imperious tone: "Death! come here."

The panther rose, but so dragged herself along that her belly and the bend of her legs touched the ground. She was three feet high, and nearly five in length; her elastic and fleshy spine, the sinews of her thighs as well developed as those of a race-horse, her deep chest, her enormous jutting shoulders, the nerve and muscle in her short, thick paws - all announced that this terrible animal united vigor with suppleness, and strength with agility.

Morok, with his iron wand still extended in the direction of the cage, made a step towards the panther. The panther made a stride towards the Prophet. Morok stopped; Death stopped also.

At this moment the tiger, Judas, to whom Morok's back was turned, bounded violently in his cage, as if jealous of the attention, which his master paid to the panther. He growled hoarsely, and, raising his head, showed the under-part of his redoubtable triangular jaw, and his broad chest of a dirty white, with which blended the copper color, streaked with black, of his sides; his tail, like a huge red serpent, with rings of ebony, now clung to his flanks, now lashed them with a slow and continuous movement: his eyes, of a transparent, brilliant green, were fixed upon the Prophet.

Such was the influence of this man over his animals, that Judas almost immediately ceased growling, as if frightened at his own temerity; but his respiration continued loud and deep. Morok turned his face towards him, and examined him very attentively during some seconds. The panther, no longer subject to the influence of her master's look, slunk back to crouch in the shade.

A sharp cracking, in sudden breaks, like that which great animals make in gnawing hard substances, was now heard from the cage of the lion. It drew the attention of the Prophet, who, leaving the tiger, advanced towards the other den.

Nothing could be seen of the lion but his monstrous croup of a reddish yellow. His thighs were gathered under him, and his thick mane served entirely to conceal his head. But by the tension and movement of the muscles of his loins, and the curving of his backbone, it was easy to perceive that he was making violent efforts with his throat and his forepaws. The Prophet approached the cage with same uneasiness, fearing that, notwithstanding his orders, Goliath had given the lion some bones to gnaw. To assure himself of it, he said in a quick and firm voice: "Cain!"

The lion did not change his position.

"Cain! come here!" repeated Morok in a louder tone. The appeal was useless; the lion did not move, and the noise continued.

"Cain! come here!" said the Prophet a third time; but, as he pronounced these words, he applied the end of the glowing bar to the haunch of the lion.

Scarcely did the light track of smoke appear on the reddish hide of Cain, when, with a spring of incredible agility, he turned and threw himself against the grating, not crouching, but at a single bound - upright, superb, terrifying. The Prophet being at the angle of the cage, Cain, in his fury, had raised himself sideways to face his master, and, leaning his huge flank against the bars, thrust between them his enormous fore leg, which, with his swollen muscles, was as large as

Goliath's thigh.

"Cain! down!" said the Prophet, approaching briskly.

The lion did not obey immediately. His lips, curling with rage, displayed fangs as long, as large, and as pointed as the tusks of a wild boar. But Morok touched those lips with the end of the burning metal; and, as he felt the smart, followed by an unexpected summons of his master, the lion, not daring to roar, uttered a hollow growl, and his great body sank down at once in an attitude of submission and fear.

The Prophet took down the lantern to see what Cain had been gnawing. It was one of the planks from the floor of his den, which he had succeeded in tearing up, and was crunching between his teeth in the extremity of his hunger. For a few moments the most profound silence reigned in the menagerie. The Prophet, with his hands behind his back, went from one cage to the other, observing the animals with a restless contemplative look, as if he hesitated to make between them an important and difficult choice.

From time to time he listened at the great door of the shed, which opened on the court-yard of the inn. At length this door turned on its hinges, and Goliath appeared, his clothes dripping with water.

"Well! is it done?" said the Prophet.

"Not without trouble. Luckily, the night is dark, it blows hard, and it pours with rain."

"Then there is no suspicion?"

"None, master. Your information was good. The door of the cellar opens on the fields, just under the window of the lasses. When you whistled to let me know it was time, I crept out with a stool I had provided; I put it up against the wall, and mounted upon it; with my six feet, that made nine, and I could lean my elbows on the window-ledge; I took the shutter in one hand, and the haft of my knife in the other, and, whilst I broke two of the panes, I pushed the shutter with all my might."

"And they thought it was the wind?"

"Yes, they thought it was the wind. You see, the 'brute' is not such a brute, after all. That done, I crept back into my cellar, carrying my stool with me. In a little time, I heard the voice of the old man; it was well I had made haste."

"Yes, when I whistled to you, he had just entered the supper-room. I thought he would have been longer."

"That man's not built to remain long at supper," said the giant, contemptuously. "Some moments after the panes had been broken, the old man opened the window, and called his dog, saying: 'Jump out!' - I went and hid myself at the further end of the cellar, or that infernal dog would have scented me through the door."

"The dog is now shut up in the stable with the old man's horse."

"Go on!"

"When I heard them close shutter and window, I came out of my cellar, replaced my stool, and again mounted upon it. Unfastening the shutter, I opened it without noise, but the two broken panes were stopped up with the skirts of a pelisse. I heard talking, but I could see nothing; so I moved the pelisse a little, and then I could see the two lasses in bed opposite to me, and the old man sitting down with his back to where I stood."

"But the knapsack - the knapsack? - That is the most important."

"The knapsack was near the window, on a table, by the side of a lamp; I could have reached it by stretching out my arm."

"What did you hear said?"

"As you told me to think only of the knapsack, I can only remember what concerns the knapsack. The old man said he had some papers in it - the letter of a general - his money - his cross."

"Good - what next?"

"As it was difficult for me to keep the pelisse away from the hole, it slipped through my fingers. In trying to get hold of it again, I put my hand too much forward. One of the lasses saw it, and screamed out, pointing to the window."

"Dolt!" exclaimed the Prophet, becoming pale with rage, "you have ruined all."

"Stop a bit! there is nothing broken yet. When I heard the scream, I jumped down from my stool, and got back into the cellar; as the dog was no longer about, I left the door ajar, so that I could hear them open the window, and see, by the light, that the old man was looking out with the lamp; but he could find no ladder, and the window was too high for any man of common size to reach it!"

"He will have thought, like the first time, that it was the wind. You are less awkward than I imagined."

"The wolf has become a fox, as you said. Knowing where the knapsack was to be found with the money and the papers, and not being able to do more for the moment, I came away - and here I am."

"Go upstairs and fetch me the longest pike."

"Yes, master."

Eugene Sue

"And the red blanket."

"Yes, master."

"Go!"

Goliath began to mount the ladder; half-way up he stopped. "Master," said he, "may I not bring down a bit of meat for Death? - you will see that she'll bear me malice; she puts it all down to my account; she never forgets, and on the first occasion -"

"The pike and the cloth!" repeated the Prophet, in an imperious tone. And whilst Goliath, swearing to himself, proceeded to execute his instructions, Morok opened the great door of the shed, looked out into the yard, and listened.

"Here's the pike and the cloth," said the giant, as he descended the ladder with the articles. "Now what must I do next?"

"Return to the cellar, mount once more by the window, and when the old man leaves the room -"

"Who will make him leave the room?"

"Never mind! he will leave it."

"What next?"

"You say the lamp is near the window?"

"Quite near - on the table next to the knapsack."

"Well, then, as soon as the old man leaves the room, push open the window, throw down the lamp, and if you accomplish cleverly what remains to do - the ten florins are yours - you remember it all?"

"Yes, yes."

"The girls will be so frightened by the noise and darkness, that they will remain dumb with terror."

"Make yourself easy! The wolf turned into a fox; why not a serpent?"

"There is yet something."

"Well, what now?"

"The roof of this shed is not very high, the window of the loft is easy of access, the night is dark - instead of returning by the door -"

"I will come in at the window."

"Ay, and without noise."

"Like a regular snake!" and the giant departed.

"Yes!" said the Prophet to himself, after a long silence, "these means are sure. It was not for me to hesitate. A blind and obscure instrument, I know not the motives of the orders I have received: but from the recommendations which accompany them - but from the position of him who sends them - immense interests must be involved - interests connected with all that is highest and greatest upon earth! - And yet how can these two girls, almost beggars, how can this wretched soldier represent such interests? - No matter," added he, with humility; "I am the arm which acts - it is for the head, which thinks and orders, to answer for its work."

Soon after the Prophet left the shed, carrying with him the red cloth, and directed his steps towards the little stable that contained Jovial. The crazy door, imperfectly secured by a latch, was easily opened. At sight of a stranger Spoil-sport threw himself upon him; but his teeth encountered the iron leggings of the Prophet, who, in spite of the efforts of the dog took Jovial by his halter, threw the blanket over his head to prevent his either seeing or smelling, and led him from the stable into the interior of the menagerie, of which he closed the door.

CHAPTER X

THE SURPRISE

The orphans, after reading the journal of their father, remained for some moments silent, sad, and pensive, contemplating the leaves yellowed by time. Dagobert, also plunged in a reverie, thought of his wife and son, from whom he had been so long separated, and hoped soon to see again.

The soldier was the first to break the silence, which had lasted for several minutes. Taking the leaves from the hand of Blanche, he folded them carefully, put them into his pocket, and thus addressed the orphans:

"Courage, my children! you see what a brave father you have. Think only of the pleasure of greeting him, and remember always the name of the gallant youth, to whom you will owe that pleasure - for without him your father would have been killed in India."

"Djalma! we shall never forget him," said Rose.

"And if our guardian angel Gabriel should return," added Blanche, "we will ask him to watch over Djalma as over ourselves."

"Very well, my children; I am sure that you will forget nothing that concerns good feeling. But to return to the traveller, who came to visit your poor mother in Siberia, he had seen the

Eugene Sue

general a month after the events of which you have read, and at a moment when he was about to enter on a new campaign against the English. It was then that your father entrusted him with the papers and medal."

"But of what use will this medal be to us, Dagobert?"

"And what is the meaning of these words engraved upon it?" added Rose, as she drew it from her bosom.

"Why it means, my children, that on the 13th of February, 1832, we must be at No. 3, Rue Saint Francois, Paris."

"But what are we to do there?"

"Your poor mother was seized so quickly with her last illness, that she was unable to tell me. All I know is, that this medal came to her from her parents, and that it had been a relic preserved in her family for more than a century."

"And how did our father get it?"

"Among the articles which had been hastily thrown into the coach, when he was removed by force from Warsaw, was a dressing-case of your mother's, in which was contained this medal. Since that time the general had been unable to send it back, having no means of communicating with us, and not even knowing where we were."

"This medal is, then, of great importance to us?"

"Unquestionably; for never, during fifteen years, had I seen your mother so happy, as on the day the traveller brought it back to her. 'Now,' said she to me, in the presence of the stranger, and with tears of joy in her eyes, 'now may my children's future be brilliant as their life has hitherto been miserable. I will entreat of the governor of Siberia permission to go to France with my daughters; it will perhaps be thought I have been sufficiently punished, by fifteen years of exile, and the confiscation of my property. Should they refuse, I will remain here; but they will at least allow me to send my children to France, and you must accompany them, Dagobert. You shall set out immediately, for much time has been already lost; and, if you were not to arrive before the 13th of next February, this cruel separation and toilsome journey would have been all in vain.'"

"Suppose we were one day after?"

"Your mother told me that if we arrived the 14th instead of the 13th, it would be too late. She also gave me a thick letter, to put into the post for France, in the first town we should pass through - which I have done."

"And do you think we shall be at Paris in time?"

"I hope so; still, if you are strong enough, we must sometimes make forced marches - for, if we only travel our five leagues a day, and that without accident, we shall scarcely reach Paris until the beginning of February, and it is better to be a little beforehand."

"But as father is in - India, and condemned to death if he return to France, when shall we see him?"

"And where shall we see him?"

"Poor children! there are so many things you have yet to learn. When the traveller quitted him, the general could not return to France, but now he can do so."

"And why is that?"

"Because the Bourbons, who had banished him, were themselves turned out last year. The news must reach India, and your father will certainly come to meet you at Paris, because he expects that you and your mother will be there on the 13th of next February."

Eugene Sue

"Ah! now I understand how we may hope to see him," said Rose with a sigh.

"Do you know the name of this traveller, Dagobert?"

"No, my children; but whether called Jack or John, he is a good sort. When he left your mother, she thanked him with tears for all his kindness and devotion to the general, herself, and the children; but he pressed her hands in his, and said to her, in so gentle a voice that I could not help being touched by it: 'Why do you thank me? Did He not Say - LOVE YE ONE ANOTHER!'"

"Who is that, Dagobert?"

"Yes, of whom did the traveller speak?"

"I know nothing about it; only the manner in which he pronounced those words struck me, and they were the last he spoke."

"Love one another!" repeated Rose, thoughtfully.

"How beautiful are those words!" added Blanche.

"And whither was the traveller going?"

"Far, very far into the North, as he told your mother. When she saw him depart, she said to me: 'His mild, sad talk has affected me even to tears; whilst I listened to him, I seemed to be growing better - I seemed to love my husband and my children more - and yet, to judge by the expression of his countenance, one would think that this stranger had never either smiled or wept!' She and I watched him from the door as long as we could follow him with our eyes; he carried his head down, and his walk was slow, calm, and firm; one might fancy that he counted his steps. And, talking of steps, I remarked yet another thing."

"What was it, Dagobert?"

"You know that the road which led to our house way, always damp, because of the overflowing of the little spring."

"Yes."

"Well, then, the mark of the traveller's footsteps remained in the clay, and I saw that he had nails under his shoe in the form of a cross."

"How in the form of a cross?"

"Look!" said Dagobert, placing the tip of his finger seven times on the coverlet of the bed; "they were arrange: thus beneath his heel:"

```
            *
         *  *  *
            *
            *
            *
```

"You see it forms a cross."

"What could it mean, Dagobert?"

"Chance, perhaps - yes, chance - and yet, in spite of myself, this confounded cross left behind him struck me as a bad omen, for hardly was he gone when misfortune after misfortune fell upon us."

"Alas! the death of our mother!"

"Yes - but, before that, another piece of ill-luck. You had not yet returned, and she was writing her petition to ask leave to go to France or to send you there, when I heard the gallop of a horse. It was a courier from the governor general of Siberia. He brought us orders to change our residence; within three days we were to join other condemned persons, and be removed with them four hundred leagues further north. Thus, after fifteen years of exile, they redoubled in cruelty towards your mother."

"Why did they thus torment her?"

"One would think that some evil genius was at work against her. A few days later, the traveller would no longer have found us at Milosk; and if he had joined us further on, it would have been too far for the medal and papers to be of use - since, having set out almost immediately, we shall hardly arrive in time at Paris. 'If they had some interest to prevent me and my children from going to France,' said your mother, 'they would act just as they have done. To banish us four hundred leagues further, is to render impossible this journey, of which the term is fixed.' And the idea overwhelmed her with grief."

"Perhaps it was this unexpected sorrow that was the cause of her sudden illness."

"Alas! no, my children; it was that infernal cholera, who arrives without giving you notice - for he too is a great traveller - and strikes you down like a thunderbolt. Three hours after the traveller had left us, when you returned quite pleased and gay from the forest, with your large bunches of wild-flowers for your mother, she was already in the last agony, and hardly to be recognized. The cholera had broken out in the village, and that evening five persons died of it. Your mother had only time to hang the medal about your neck, my dear little Rose, to recommend you both to my care, and to beg that we should set out immediately. When she was gone, the new order of exile could not apply to you; and I obtained permission from the governor to take my departure with you for France, according to the last wishes - "

The soldier could not finish the sentence; he covered his eyes with his hand, whilst the orphans embraced him sobbing.

"Oh! but," resumed Dagobert, with pride, after a moment of painful silence, "it was then that you showed yourselves the brave daughters of the general. Notwithstanding the danger, it was impossible to tear you from your mother's bedside; you remained with her to the last, you closed her eyes, you watched there all night, and you would not leave the village till you had seen me plant the little wooden cross over the grave I had dug for her."

Dagobert paused abruptly. A strange, wild neighing, mingled with ferocious roarings, made the soldier start from his seat. He grew pale, and cried: "It is Jovial! my horse! What are they doing to my horse?" With that, opening the door he rushed down the stairs precipitately.

The two sisters clung together, so terrified at the sudden departure of the soldier, that they saw not an enormous hand pass through the broken panes, unfasten the catch of the window, push it violently open, and throw down the lamp placed on the little table, on which was the soldiers's knapsack. The orphans thus found themselves plunged into complete darkness.

CHAPTER XI

JOVIAL and DEATH

Morok had led Jovial into the middle of the menagerie, and then removed the cloth which prevented him from seeing and smelling. Scarcely had the tiger, lion, and panther caught a glimpse of him than they threw themselves, half famished, against the bars of their dens.

The horse struck with stupor, his neck stretched out, his eye fixed, and trembling through all his limbs, appeared as if nailed to the ground; an abundant icy sweat rolled suddenly down his flanks. The lion and the tiger uttered fearful roarings, and struggled violently in their dens. The panther did not roar, but her mute rage was terrific.

With a tremendous bound, at the risk of breaking her skull, she sprang from the back of the cage against the bars; then, still mute, still furious, she crawled back to the extreme corner of the den, and with a new spring, as impetuous as it was blind, she again strove to force out the iron grating. Three times had she thus bounded - silent, appalling - when the horse, passing from the immobility of stupor to the wild agony of fear, neighed long and loud, and rushed in desperation at the door by which he had entered. Finding it closed he hung his head, bent his knees a little, and rubbed his nostrils against the opening left between the ground and the bottom of the door, as if he wished to inhale the air from the outside; then, more and more affrighted, he began to neigh with redoubled force, and struck out violently with his fore-feet.

At the moment when Death was about once more to make her spring, the Prophet approached her cage. The heavy bolt which secured the grating was pushed from its staple by the pike of the brute-tamer, and, in another second, Morok was half way up the ladder that communicated with the loft.

The roaring of the lion and tiger, mingled with the neighing of Jovial, now resounded through all parts of the inn. The panther had again thrown herself furiously on the grating, and this time yielding with one spring, she was in the middle of the shed.

The light of the lantern was reflected from the glossy ebon of her hide, spotted with stains of a duller black. For an instant she remained motionless, crouching upon her thick-set limbs, with her head close to the floor, as if calculating the distance of the leap by which she was to reach the horse; then suddenly she darted upon him.

On seeing her break from her cage Jovial had thrown himself violently against the door, which was made to open inwards, and leaned against it with all his might, as though he would force it down. Then, at the moment when Death took her leap, he reared up in almost an erect position; but she, rapid as lightning, had fastened upon his throat and hung there, whilst at the same time she buried the sharp claws of her fore-feet in his chest. The jugular vein of the horse opened; a torrent of bright red blood spouted forth beneath the tooth of the panther, who, now supporting herself on her hind legs, squeezed her victim up against the door, whilst she dug into his flank with her claws, and laid bare the palpitating flesh. Then his half-strangled neighing became awful.

Suddenly these words resounded: "Courage, Jovial! - I am at hand! Courage!"

It was the voice of Dagobert, who was exhausting himself in

Eugene Sue

desperate exertions to force open the door that concealed this sanguinary struggle. "Jovial!" cried the soldier, "I am here. Help! Help!"

At the sound of that friendly and well-known voice, the poor animal, almost at its last gasp, strove to turn its head in the direction whence came the accents of his master, answered him with a plaintive neigh, and, sinking beneath the efforts of the panther, fell prostrate, first on its knees, then upon its flank, so that its backbone lay right across the door, and still prevented its being opened. And now all was finished. The panther, squatting down upon the horse, crushed him with all her paws, and, in spite of some last faint kicks, buried her bloody snout in his body.

"Help! help! my horse!" cried Dagobert, as he vainly shook the door. "And no arms!" he added with rage; "no arms!"

"Take care!" exclaimed the brute-tamer, who appeared at the window of the loft; "do not attempt to enter it might cost you your life. My panther is furious."

"But my horse! my horse!" cried Dagobert, in a voice of agony.

"He must have strayed from his stable during the night, and pushed open the door of the shed. At sight of him the panther must have broken out of her cage and seized him. You are answerable for all the mischief that may ensue," added the brute-tamer, with a menacing air; "for I shall have to run the greatest danger, to make Death return to her den."

"But my horse! only save my horse!" cried Dagobert, in a tone of hopeless supplication.

The Prophet disappeared from the window.

The roaring of the animals and the shouts of Dagobert, had roused from sleep every one in the White Falcon. Here and there lights were seen moving and windows were thrown open hurriedly. The servants of the inn soon appeared in the yard with lanterns, and surrounding Dagobert, inquired of him what had happened.

"My horse is there," cried the soldier, continuing to shake the door, "and one of that scoundrel's animals has escaped from its cage."

At these words the people of the inn, already terrified by the frightful roaring, fled from the spot and ran to inform the host. The soldier's anguish may be conceived, as pale, breathless, with his ear close to the chink of the door, he stood listening. By degrees the roaring had ceased, and nothing was heard but low growls, accompanied by the stern voice of the Prophet, repeating in harsh, abrupt accents: "Death! come here! Death!"

The night was profoundly dark, and Dagobert did not perceive Goliath, who, crawling carefully along the tiled roof entered the loft by the attic window.

And now the gate of the court-yard was again opened, and the landlord of the inn appeared, followed by a number of men. Armed with a carbine, he advanced with precaution; his people carried staves and pitchforks.

"What is the row here?" said he, as he approached Dagobert. "What a hubbub in my house! The devil take wild beast showmen, and negligent fellows who don't know how to tie a horse to the manger! If your beast is hurt, so much the worse for you; you should have taken more care of it."

Instead of replying to these reproaches, the soldier, who still listened attentively to what was going on in the shed, made a sign to entreat silence. Suddenly a ferocious roar was heard, followed by a loud scream from the Prophet; and, almost immediately after, the panther howled piteously.

"You are no doubt the cause of some great accident," said the frightened host to the soldier; "did you not hear that cry? Morok is, perhaps, dangerously wounded."

Dagobert was about to answer, when the door opened, and Goliath appeared on the threshold.

"You may enter now," said he; "the danger is over."

The interior of the menagerie presented a singular spectacle. The Prophet, pale, and scarcely able to conceal his agitation beneath an apparent air of calmness, was kneeling some paces from the cage of the panther, in the attitude of one absorbed in himself; the motion of his lips indicating that he was praying. At sight of the host and the people of the inn, he rose, and said in a solemn voice: "I thank thee, my Preserver, that I have been able to conquer, by the strength which Thou hast given me."

Then folding his arms, with haughty brow and imperious glance, he seemed to enjoy the triumph he had achieved over Death, who, stretched on the bottom of her den, continued to utter plaintive howlings. The spectators of this scene, ignorant that the pelisse of the brute-tamer covered a complete suit of armor, and attributing the cries of the panther solely to fear, were struck with astonishment and admiration at the intrepidity and almost supernatural power of this man. A few steps behind him stood Goliath, leaning upon the ashen pikestaff. Finally, not far from the cage, in the midst of a pool of blood, lay the dead body of Jovial.

At sight of the blood-stained and torn remains, Dagobert stood motionless, and his rough countenance assumed an expression of the deepest grief: then, throwing himself on his knees, he lifted the head of Jovial; and when he saw those dull, glassy, and half-closed eyes, once so bright and intelligent, as they turned towards a much-loved master, the soldier could not suppress an exclamation of bitter anguish. Forgetting his anger, forgetting the deplorable consequences of this accident, so fatal to the interests of the two maidens, who would thus be prevented from continuing their journey - he thought only of the horrible death of his poor old horse, the ancient companion of his fatigues and wars, the faithful animal, twice wounded like himself, and from whom for so many years he had never been separated. This poignant emotion was so cruelly, so affectingly visible in the soldier's countenance, that the landlord and his people felt themselves for a moment touched with pity, as they gazed on the tall veteran kneeling beside his dead horse.

But, when following the course of his regrets, he thought how Jovial had also been the companion of his exile, how the mother of the orphans had formerly (like her daughters) undertaken a toilsome journey with the aid of this unfortunate animal, the fatal consequences of his loss presented themselves on a sudden to his mind. Then, fury succeeding to grief, he rose, with anger flashing from his eyes, and threw himself on the Prophet; with one hand he seized him by the throat, and with the other administered five or six heavy blows, which fell harmlessly on the coat of mail.

"Rascal! you shall answer to me for my horse's death!" said the soldier, as he continued his correction. Morok, light and sinewy, could not struggle with advantage against Dagobert, who, aided by his tall stature, still displayed extraordinary vigor. It needed the intervention of Goliath and the landlord to rescue the Prophet from the hands of the old grenadier. After some moments, they succeeded in separating the two champions. Morok was white with rage. It needed new efforts to prevent his seizing the pike to attack Dagobert.

"It is abominable!" cried the host, addressing the soldier, who pressed his clinched fists in despair against his bald forehead. "You expose this good man to be devoured by his beasts, and then you wish to beat him into the bargain. Is this fitting conduct for a graybeard? Shall we have to fetch the police? You showed yourself more reasonable in the early part of the evening."

These words recalled the soldier to himself. He regretted his

Eugene Sue

impetuosity the more, as the fact of his being a stranger might augment the difficulty of his position. It was necessary above all to obtain the price of his horse, so as to be enabled to continue his journey, the success of which might be compromised by a single day's delay. With a violent effort, therefore, he succeeded in restraining his wrath.

"You are right - I was too hasty," said he to the host, in an agitated voice, which he tried to make as calm as possible. "I had not the same patience as before. But ought not this man be responsible for the loss of my horse? I make you judge in the matter."

"Well, then, as judge, I am not of your opinion. All this has been your own fault. You tied up your horse badly, and he strayed by chance into this shed, of which no doubt the door was half-open," said the host, evidently taking the part of the brute-tamer.

"It was just as you say," answered Goliath. "I can remember it. I left the door ajar, that the beasts might have some air in the night. The cages were well shut, and there was no danger."

"Very true," said one of the standers-by.

"It was only the sight of the horse," added another, "that made the panther furious, so as to break out of its cage."

"It is the Prophet who has the most right to complain," observed a third.

"No matter what this or that person says," returned Dagobert, whose patience was beginning to fail him, "I say, that I must have either money or a horse on the instant - yes, on the instant - for I wish to quit this unlucky house."

"And I say, it is you that must indemnify me," cried Morok, who had kept this stage-trick for the last, and who now exhibited his left hand all bloody, having hitherto concealed it beneath the sleeve of his pelisse. "I shall perhaps be disabled for life," he added; "see what a wound the panther has made here!"

Without having the serious character that the Prophet ascribed to it, the wound was a pretty deep one. This last argument gained for him the general sympathy. Reckoning no doubt upon this incident, to secure the winning of a cause that he now regarded as his own, the host said to the hostler: "There is only one way to make a finish. It is to call up the burgomaster, and beg him to step here. He will decide who is right or wrong."

"I was just going to propose it to you," said the soldier, "for, after all, I cannot take the law into my own hands."

"Fritz, run to the burgomaster's!" - and the hustler started in all haste. His master, fearing to be compromised by the examination of the soldier, whose papers he had neglected to ask for on his arrival, said to him: "The burgomaster will be in a very bad humor, to be disturbed so late. I have no wish to suffer by it, and I must therefore beg you to go and fetch me your papers, to see if they are in rule. I ought to have made you show them, when you arrived here in the evening."

"They are upstairs in my knapsack; you shall have them," answered the soldier - and turning away his head, and putting his hand before his eyes, as he passed the dead body of Jovial, he went out to rejoin the sisters.

The Prophet followed him with a glance of triumph, and said to himself: "There he goes! - without horse, without money, without papers. I could not do more - for I was forbidden to do more - I was to act with as much cunning as possible and preserve appearances. Now every one will think this soldier in the wrong. I can at least answer for it, that he will not continue his journey for some days - since such great interests appear to depend on his arrest, and that of the young girls."

A quarter of an hour after this reflection of the brute-tamer,

Karl, Goliath's comrade, left the hiding-place where his master had concealed him during the evening, and set out for Leipsic, with a letter which Morok had written in haste, and which Karl, on his arrival, was to put immediately into the post.

The address of this letter was as follows:

"A Monsieur Rodin, Rue du Milieu-des-Ursins, No, 11, A Paris, France."

CHAPTER XII

THE BURGOMASTER

Dagobert's anxiety increased every moment. Certain that his horse had not entered the shed of its own accord, he attributed the event which had taken place to the spite of the brute-tamer; but he sought in vain for the motive of this wretch's animosity, and he reflected with dismay, that his cause, however just, would depend on the good or bad humor of a judge dragged from his slumbers and who might be ready to condemn upon fallacious appearances.

Fully determined to conceal, as long as possible, from the orphans the fresh misfortunes, which had befallen them, he was proceeding to open the door of their chamber, when he stumbled over Spoil-sport - for the dog had run back to his post, after vainly trying to prevent the Prophet from leading away Jovial. "Luckily the dog has returned; the poor little things have been well guarded," said the soldier, as he opened the door. To his great surprise, the room was in utter darkness.

"My children," cried he, "why are you without a light?" There was no answer. In terror he groped his way to the bed, and took the hand of one of the sisters; the hand was cold as ice.

"Rose, my children!" cried he. "Blanche! Give me some answer! you frighten me." Still the same silence continued; the hand which he held remained cold and powerless, and yielded passively to his touch.

Eugene Sue

Just then, the moon emerged from the black clouds that surrounded her, and threw sufficient light into the little room, and upon the bed, which faced the window, for the soldier to see that the two sisters had fainted. The bluish light of the moon added to the paleness of the orphans; they held each other in a half embrace, and Rose had buried her head on Blanche's bosom.

"They must have fainted through fear," exclaimed Dagobert, running to fetch his gourd. "Poor things! after a day of so much excitement, it is not surprising." And moistening the corner of a handkerchief with a few drops of brandy, the soldier knelt beside the bed, gently chafed the temples of the two sisters, and held the linen, wet with the spirituous liquor, to their little pink nostrils.

Still on his knees, and bending his dark, anxious face over the orphans, he waited some moments before again resorting to the only restorative in his power. A slight shiver of Rose gave him renewed hope; the young girl turned her head on the pillow with a sigh; then she started, and opened her eyes with an expression of astonishment and alarm; but, not immediately recognizing Dagobert, she exclaimed: "Oh, sister!" and threw herself into the arms of Blanche.

The latter also was beginning to experience the effect of the soldier's care. The exclamation of Rose completely roused her from her lethargy, and she clung to her sister, again sharing the fright without knowing its cause.

"They've come to - that's the chief point," said Dagobert, "now we shall soon get rid of these foolish fears." Then softening his voice, he added: "Well, my children, courage? You are better. It is I who am here - me, Dagobert!"

The orphans made a hasty movement, and, turning towards the soldier their sweet faces, which were still full of dismay and agitation, they both, by a graceful impulse, extended their arms to him and cried: "It is you, Dagobert - then we are safe!"

"Yes, my children, it is I," said the veteran, taking their hands in his, and pressing them joyfully. "So you have been much frightened during my absence?"

"Oh, frightened to death!"

"If you knew - oh, goodness! if you knew -"

"But the lamp is extinguished - why is that?"

"We did not do it."

"Come - recover yourselves, poor children, and tell me all about it. I have no good opinion of this inn; but, luckily, we shall soon leave it. It was an ill wind that blew me hither - though, to be sure, there was no other in the village. But what has happened?"

"You were hardly gone, when the window flew open violently, and the lamp and table fell together with a loud crash."

"Then our courage failed - we screamed and clasped each other, for we thought we could hear some one moving in the room."

"And we were so frightened, that we fainted away."

Unfortunately, persuaded that it was the violence of the wind which had already broken the glass, and shaken the window, Dagobert attributed this second accident to the same cause as the first, thinking that he had not properly secured the fastening and that the orphans had been deceived by a false alarm. "Well, well - it is over now," said he to them: "Calm yourselves, and don't think of it any more."

"But why did you leave us so hastily, Dagobert?"

"Yes, now I remember - did we not hear a great noise, sister, and see Dagobert run to the staircase, crying: 'My horse! what are they doing to my horse?'"

"It was then Jovial who neighed?"

These questions renewed the anguish of the soldier; he feared to answer them, and said, with a confused air: "Yes - Jovial neighed - but it was nothing. By the by, we must have a light here. Do you know where I put my flint and steel last evening? Well, I have lost my senses; it is here in my pocket. Luckily, too, we have a candle, which I am going to light; I want to look in my knapsack for some papers I require."

Dagobert struck a few sparks, obtained a light, and saw that the window was indeed open, the table thrown down, and the lamp lying by the side of the knapsack. He shut the window, set the little table on its feet again, placed the knapsack upon it, and began to unbuckle this last in order to take out his portfolio, which had been deposited along with his cross and purse, in a kind of pocket between the outside and the lining. The straps had been readjusted with so much care, that there was no appearance of the knapsack having been disturbed; but when the soldier plunged his hand into the pocket above-mentioned, he found it empty. Struck with consternation, he grew pale, and retreated a step, crying: "How is this? - Nothing!"

"What is the matter?" said Blanche. He made her no answer. Motionless, he leaned against the table, with his hand still buried in the pocket. Then, yielding to a vague hope - for so cruel a reality did not appear possible - he hastily emptied the contents of the knapsack on the table - his poor half-worn clothes - his old uniform-coat of the horse-grenadiers of the Imperial Guard, a sacred relic for the soldiers - but, turn and return them as he would, he found neither his purse, nor the portfolio that contained his papers, the letters of General Simon, and his cross.

In vain, with that serious childishness which always accompanies a hopeless search, he took the knapsack by the two ends, and shook it vigorously; nothing came out. The orphans looked on with uneasiness, not understanding his silence or his movements, for his back was turned to them. Blanche ventured to say to him in a timid voice: "What ails you - you don't answer us. - What is it you are looking for in your knapsack?"

Still mute, Dagobert searched his own person, turned out all his pockets - nothing! - For the first time in his life, perhaps, his two children, as he called them, had spoken to him without receiving a reply. Blanche and Rose felt the big tears start into their eyes; thinking that the soldier was angry, they darst not again address him.

"No, no! it is impossible - no!" said the veteran, pressing his hand to his forehead, and seeking in his memory where he might have put those precious objects, the loss of which he could not yet bring himself to believe. A sudden beam of joy flashed from his eyes. He ran to a chair, and took from it the portmanteau of the orphans; it contained a little linen, two black dresses, and a small box of white wood, in which were a silk handkerchief that had belonged to their mother, two locks of her hair, and a black ribbon she had worn round her neck. The little she possessed had been seized by the Russian government, in pursuance of the confiscation. Dagobert searched and researched every article - peeped into all the corners of the portmanteau - still nothing!

This time, completely worn out, leaning against the table, the strong, energetic man felt himself giving way. His face was burning, yet bathed in a cold sweat; his knees trembled under him. It is a common saying, that drowning men will catch at straws; and so it is with the despair that still clings to some shred of hope. Catching at a last chance - absurd, insane, impossible - he turned abruptly towards the orphans, and said to them, without considering the alteration in his voice and features: "I did not give them to you - to keep for me? - speak?"

Instead of answering, Rose and Blanche, terrified at his paleness and the expression of his countenance, uttered a cry. "Good heavens! what is the matter with you?" murmured Rose.

"Have you got them - yes, or no?" cried in a voice of thunder the unfortunate, distracted man. "If you have not - I'll take the first knife I meet with, and stick it into my body!"

"Alas! You are so good: pardon us if we have done anything to afflict you! You love us so much, you would not do us any harm." The orphans began to weep, as they stretched forth their hands in supplication towards the soldier.

He looked at them with haggard eye, without even seeing them; till, as the delusion passed away, the reality presented itself to his mind with all its terrible consequences. Then he clasped his hands together, fell on his knees before the bed of the orphans, leaned his forehead upon it, and amid his convulsive sobs - for the man of iron sobbed like a child - these broken words were audible: "Forgive me - forgive! - I do not know how it can be! - Oh! what a misfortune! - what a misfortune! – Forgive me!"

At this outbreak of grief, the cause of which they understood not, but which in such a man was heart-rending, the two sisters wound their arms about his old gray head, and exclaimed amid their tears: "Look at us! Only tell us what is the matter with you? - Is it our fault?"

At this instant, the noise of footsteps resounded from the stairs, mingled with the barking of Spoil-sport, who had remained outside the door. The nearer the steps approached, the more furious became the barking; it was no doubt accompanied with hostile demonstrations, for the host was heard to cry out in an angry tone: "Hollo! you there! Call off your dog, or speak to him. It is Mr. Burgomaster who is coming up."

"Dagobert - do you hear? - it is the burgomaster," said Rose.

"They are coming upstairs - a number of people," resumed Blanche.

The word burgomaster recalled whatever had happened to the mind of Dagobert, and completed, so to express it, the picture of his terrible position. His horse was dead, he had neither papers nor money, and a day, a single day's detention, might defeat the last hope of the sisters, and render useless this long and toilsome journey.

Men of strong minds, and the veteran was of the number, prefer great perils, positions of danger accurately defined, to the vague anxieties which precede a settled misfortune. Guided by his good sense and admirable devotion, Dagobert understood at once, that his only resource was now in the justice of the burgomaster, and that all his efforts should tend to conciliate the favor of that magistrate. He therefore dried his eyes with the sheet, rose from the ground, erect, calm, and resolute, and said to the orphans: "Fear nothing, my children; it is our deliverer who is at hand."

"Will you call off your dog or no?" cried the host, still detained on the stairs by Spoil-sport, who, as a vigilant sentinel, continued to dispute the passage. "Is the animal mad, I say? Why don't you tie him up? Have you not caused trouble enough in my house? I tell you, that Mr. Burgomaster is waiting to examine you in your turn, for he has finished with Morok."

Dagobert drew his fingers through his gray locks and across his moustache, clasped the collar of his top-coat, and brushed the sleeves with his hand, in order to give himself the best appearance possible; for he felt that the fate of the orphans must depend on his interview with the magistrate. It was not without a violent beating of the heart, that he laid his hand upon the door-knob, saying to the young girls, who were growing more and more frightened by such a succession of events: "Hide yourselves in your bed, my children; if any one must needs enter, it shall be the burgomaster alone."

Thereupon, opening the door, the soldier stepped out on the landing place, and said: "Down, Spoil-sport! - Here!"

The dog obeyed, but with manifest repugnance. His master had to speak twice, before he would abstain from all hostile movements towards the host. This latter, with a lantern in one hand and his cap in the other, respectfully preceded the burgomaster, whose magisterial proportions were lost in the half shadows of the staircase. Behind the judge, and a few steps lower, the inquisitive faces of the people belonging to the inn were dimly visible by the light of another lantern.

Dagobert, having turned the dog into the room, shut the door after him, and advanced two steps on the landing-place, which was sufficiently spacious to hold several persons, and had in one corner a wooden bench with a back to it. The burgo-master, as he ascended the last stair, was surprised to see Dagobert close the door of the chamber, as though he wished to forbid his entrance. "Why do you shut that door?" asked he in an abrupt tone.

"First, because two girls, whom I have the charge of, are in bed in that room; secondly, because your examination would alarm them," replied Dagobert. "Sit down upon this bench, Mr. Burgomaster, and examine me here; it will not make any difference, I should think."

"And by what right," asked the judge, with a displeased air, "do you pretend to dictate to me the place of your examination?"

"Oh, I have no such pretension, Mr. Burgomaster!" said the soldier hastily, fearing above all things to prejudice the judge against him: "only, as the girls are in bed, and already much frightened, it would be a proof of your good heart to examine me where I am."

"Humph!" said the magistrate, with ill-humor; "a pretty state of things, truly! - It was much worth while to disturb me in the middle of the night. But, come, so be it; I will examine you here." Then, turning to the landlord, he added: "Put your lantern upon this bench, and leave us."

The innkeeper obeyed, and went down, followed by his people, as dissatisfied as they were at being excluded from the examination. The veteran was left alone with the magistrate.

CHAPTER XIII

THE JUDGEMENT

The worthy burgomaster of Mockern wore a cloth cap, and was enveloped in a cloak. He sat down heavily on the bench. He was a corpulent man, about sixty, with an arrogant, morose countenance; and he frequently rubbed with his red, fat fist, eyes that were still swollen and blood shot, from his having been suddenly roused from sleep.

Dagobert stood bareheaded before him, with a submissive, respectful air, holding his old foraging cap in his hands, and trying to read in the sullen physiognomy of his judge what chance there might be to interest him in his favor - that is, in favor of the orphans.

In this critical juncture, the poor soldier summoned to his aid all his presence of mind, reason, eloquence and resolution. He, who had twenty times braved death with the utmost coolness - who, calm and serene, because sincere and tried, had never quailed before the eagle-glance of the Emperor, his hero and idol - now felt himself disconcerted and trembling before the ill-humored face of a village burgomaster. Even so, a few hours before, he had submitted, impassive and resigned, to the insults of the Prophet - that he might not compromise the sacred mission with which a dying mother had entrusted him - thus showing to what a height of heroic abnegation it is possible for a simple and honest heart to attain.

"What have you to say in your justification? Come, be quick!" said the judge roughly, with a yawn of impatience.

"I have not got to justify myself - I have to make a complaint, Mr. Burgomaster," replied Dagobert in a firm voice.

"Do you think you are to teach me in what terms I am to put my questions?" exclaimed the magistrate, in so sharp a tone that the soldier reproached himself with having begun the interview so badly. Wishing to pacify his judge, he made haste to answer with submission:

"Pardon me, Mr. Burgomaster, I have ill-explained my meaning. I only wished to say that I was not wrong in this affair."

"The Prophet says the contrary."

"The Prophet?" repeated the soldier, with an air of doubt.

"The Prophet is a pious and honest man," resumed the judge, "incapable of falsehood."

"I cannot say anything upon that subject; but you are too just, and have too good a heart, Mr. Burgomaster, to condemn without hearing me. It is not a man like you that would do an injustice; oh, one can see that at a glance!"

In resigning himself thus to play the part of a courtier, Dagobert softened as much as possible his gruff voice, and strove to give to his austere countenance a smiling, agreeable, and flattering expression. "A man like you," he added, with redoubled suavity of manner, "a respectable judge like you, never shuts his ears to one side or the other."

"Ears are not in question, but eyes; and, though mine smart as if I had rubbed them with nettles, I have seen the hand of the brute-tamer, with a frightful wound on it."

"Yes, Mr. Burgomaster, it is very true; but consider, if he had shut his cages and his door, all this would not have happened."

"Not so; it is your fault. You should have fastened your horse securely to the manger."

"You are right, Mr. Burgomaster, certainly, you are right," said the soldier, in a still more affable and conciliating voice. "It is not for a poor devil like me to contradict you. But supposing my horse was let loose out of pure malice, in order that he might stray into the menagerie - you will then acknowledge that it was not my fault. That is, you will acknowledge it if you think fit," hastily added the soldier "I have no right to dictate to you in anything."

"And why the devil should any one do you this ill-turn?"

"I do not know, Mr. Burgomaster - but -"

"You do not know - well, nor I either," said the burgomaster impatiently. "Zounds! what a many words about the carcass of an old horse!"

The countenance of the soldier, losing on a sudden its expression of forced suavity, became once more severe; he answered in a grave voice, full of emotion: "My horse is dead - he is no more than a carcass - that is true; but an hour ago, though very old, he was full of life and intelligence. He neighed joyously at my voice - and, every evening, he licked the hands of the two poor children, whom he had carried all the day - as formerly he had carried their mother. Now he will never carry any one again; they will throw him to the dogs, and all will be finished. You need not have reminded me harshly of it, Mr. Burgomaster - for I loved my horse!"

By these words, pronounced with noble and touching simplicity, the burgomaster was moved in spite of himself, and regretted his hasty speech. "It is natural that you should be sorry for your horse," said he, in a less impatient tone; "but what is to be done? - It is a misfortune."

"A misfortune? - Yes, Mr. Burgomaster, a very great misfortune. The girls, who accompany me, were too weak to undertake a long journey on foot, too poor to travel in a carriage - and yet we have to arrive in Paris before the month of February. When their mother died, I promised her to take them to France, for these children have only me to take care of them."

"You are then their -"

"I am their faithful servant, Mr. Burgomaster; and now that my horse has been killed, what can I do for them? Come, you are good, you have perhaps children of your own; if, one day, they should find themselves in the position of my two little orphans - with no wealth, no resources in the world, but an old soldier who loves them, and an old horse to carry them along - if, after being very unfortunate from their birth - yes, very unfortunate, for my orphans are the daughters of exiles - they should see happiness before them at the end of a journey, and then, by the death of their horse, that journey become impossible - tell me, Mr. Burgomaster, if this would not touch your heart? Would you not find, as I do, that the loss of my horse is irreparable?"

"Certainly," answered the burgomaster, who was not ill natured at bottom, and who could not help taking part in Dagobert's emotion; "I now understand the importance of the loss you have suffered. And then your orphans interest me: how old are they?"

"Fifteen years and two months. They are twins."

"Fifteen years and two months - that is about the age of my Frederica."

"You have a young lady of that age?" cried Dagobert, once more awaking to hope; "ah, Mr. Burgomaster! I am really no

Eugene Sue

longer uneasy about my poor children. You will do us justice."

"To do justice is my duty. After all, in this affair, the faults are about equal on both sides. You tied up your horse badly, and the brute tamer left his door open. He says: 'I am wounded in the hand.' You answer: 'My horse has been killed - and, for a thousand reasons, the loss of my horse is irreparable.'"

"You make me speak better than I could ever speak on my own account, Mr. Burgomaster," said the soldier, with a humble, insinuating smile; "but 'tis what I meant to express - and, as you say yourself, Mr. Burgomaster, my horse being my whole fortune, it is only fair -"

"Exactly so," resumed the magistrate, interrupting the soldier; "your reasons are excellent. The Prophet - who is a good and pious man with all has related the facts to me in his own way; and then, you see, he is an old acquaintance. We are nearly all zealous Catholics here, and he sells to our wives such cheap and edifying little books, with chaplets and amulets of the best manufacture, at less than the prime cost. All this, you will say, has nothing to do with the affair; and you will be right in saying so: still I must needs confess that I came here with the intention -"

"Of deciding against me, eh, Mr. Burgomaster?" said Dagobert, gaining more and more confidence. "You see, you were not quite awake, and your justice had only one eye open."

"Really, master soldier," answered the judge with good humor, "it is not unlikely; for I did not conceal from Morok that I gave it in his favor. Then he said to me (very generously, by the way): 'Since you condemn my adversary, I will not aggravate his position by telling you certain things -'"

"What! against me?"

"Apparently so; but, like a generous enemy, when I told him that I should most likely condemn you to pay him damages, he said no more about it. For I will not hide from you, that, before I heard your reasons, I fully intended that you should make compensation for the Prophet's wound."

"See, Mr. Burgomaster, how the most just and able persons are subject to be deceived," said Dagobert, becoming once more the courtier; then, trying to assume a prodigiously knowing look, he added: "But such persons find out the truth at last, and are not to be made dupes of, whatever prophets may say."

This poor attempt at a jest - the first and only one, perhaps, that Dagobert had ever been guilty of - will show the extremity to which he was reduced, and the desperate efforts of all kinds he was making to conciliate the good graces of his judge. The burgomaster did not at first see the pleasantry; he was only led to perceive it by the self satisfied mien of Dagobert, and by his inquiring glance, which seemed to say: "Is it not good, eh? - I am astonished at it myself."

The magistrate began, therefore, to smile with a patronizing air, and, nodding his head, replied in the same jocular spirit: "Ha! Ha! Ha! You are right; the Prophet is out in his prophecy. You shall not pay him any damages. The faults on both sides are equal, and the injuries balance one another. He has been wounded, your horse has been killed; so you may cry quits, and have done with it."

"But how much then, do you think he owes me?" asked the soldier, with singular simplicity.

"How much?"

"Yes, Mr. Burgomaster, what sum will he have to pay me? Yes - but, before you decide, I must tell you one thing, Mr. Burgomaster. I think I shall be entitled to spend only part of the money in buying a horse. I am sure, that, in the environs of Leipsic, I could get a beast very cheap from some of the peasants; and, between ourselves, I will own to you, that, if I could meet with only a nice little donkey - I should not be over particular - I should even like it just as well; for, after my poor Jovial, the company of another horse would be painful to me. I must also tell you -"

"Hey-day!" cried the burgomaster, interrupting Dagobert, "of what money, what donkey, and what other horse are you talking? I tell you, that you owe nothing to the Prophet, and that he owes you nothing!"

"He owes me nothing?"

"You are very dull of comprehension, my good man. I repeat, that, if the Prophet's animals have killed your horse, the Prophet himself has been badly wounded; so you may cry quits. In other words, you owe him nothing, and he owes you nothing. Now do you understand?"

Dagobert, confounded, remained for some moments without answering, whilst he looked at the burgomaster with an expression of deep anguish. He saw that his judgment would again destroy all his hopes.

"But, Mr. Burgomaster," resumed he, in an agitated voice, "you are too just not to pay attention to one thing: the wound of the brute-tamer does not prevent him from continuing his trade; the death of my horse prevents me from continuing my journey; therefore, he ought to indemnify me."

The judge considered he had already done a good deal for Dagobert, in not making him responsible for the wound of the Prophet, who, as we have already said, exercised a certain influence over the Catholics of the country by the sale of his devotional treasures, and also from its being known that he was supported by some persons of eminence. The soldier's pertinacity, therefore, offended the magistrate, who, reassuming his lofty air, replied, in a chilling tone: "You will make me repent my impartiality. How is this? Instead of thanking me, you ask for more."

"But, Mr. Burgomaster, I ask only for what is just. I wish I were wounded in the hand, like the Prophet, so that I could but continue my journey."

"We are not talking of what you wish. I have pronounced sentence - there is no more to say."

"But, Mr. Burgomaster -"

"Enough, enough. Let us go to the next subject. Your papers?"

"Yes, we will speak about my papers; but I beg of you, Mr. Burgomaster, to have pity on those two children. Let us have the means to continue our journey, and -"

"I have done all I could for you - perhaps, more than I ought. Once again, your papers!"

"I must first explain to you -"

"No! No explanation - your papers! - Or would you like me to have you arrested as a vagabond?"

"Me - arrested!"

"I tell you that, if you refuse to show me your papers, it will be as if you had none. Now, those people who have no papers we take into custody till the authorities can dispose of them. Let me see your papers, and make haste! - I am in a hurry to get home."

Dagobert's position was the more distressing, as for a moment he had indulged in sanguine hope. The last blow was now added to all the veteran had suffered since the commencement of this scene, which was a cruel as well as dangerous trial, for a man of his character - upright, but obstinate - faithful, but rough and absolute - a man who, for a long time a soldier, and a victorious one, had acquired a certain despotic mariner of treating with civilians.

At these words - "your papers," Dagobert became very pale; but he tried to conceal his anguish beneath an air of assurance, which he thought best calculated to gain the magistrate's good opinion. "I will tell you all about it, Mr. Burgomaster," said he. "Nothing can be clearer. Such a thing might happen to any one. I do not look like a beggar and a vagabond, do I? And yet - you will understand, that an honest man who travels with two young girls -"

"No more words! Your papers!"

At this juncture two powerful auxiliaries arrived to the soldier's aid. The orphans, growing more and more uneasy, and hearing Dagobert still talking upon the landing-place, had risen and dressed themselves; so that just at the instant, when the magistrate said in a rough voice - "No more words! Your papers!" - Rose and Blanche holding each other by the hand, came forth from the chamber.

At sight of those charming faces, which their poor mourning vestments only rendered more interesting, the burgomaster rose from his seat, struck with surprise and admiration. By a spontaneous movement, each sister took a hand of Dagobert, and pressed close to him, whilst they regarded the magistrate with looks of mingled anxiety and candor.

It was so touching a picture, this of the old soldier presenting as it were to his judge the graceful children, with countenances full of innocence and beauty, that the burgomaster, by a sudden reaction, found himself once more disposed to sentiments of pity. Dagobert perceived it; and, still holding the orphans by the hand, he advanced towards him, and said in a feeling voice: "Look at these poor children, Mr. Burgomaster! Could I show you a better passport?" And, overcome by so many painful sensations - restrained, yet following each other in quick succession - Dagobert felt, in spite of himself, that the tears were starting to his eyes.

Though naturally rough, and rendered still more testy by the interruption of his sleep, the burgomaster was not quite deficient in sense of feeling. He perceived at once, that a man thus accompanied, ought not to inspire any great distrust. "Poor dear children!" said he, as he examined them with growing interest; "orphans so young, and they come from far -"

"From the heart of Siberia, Mr. Burgomaster, where their mother was an exile before their birth. It is now more than five months that we have been travelling on by short stages - hard enough, you will say, for children of their age. It is for them that I ask your favor and support for them against whom everything seems to combine to-day for, only just now, when I went to look for my papers, I could not find in my knapsack the portfolio in which they were, along with my purse and cross - for you must know, Mr. Burgomaster - pardon me, if I say it - 'tis not from vain glory - but I was decorated by the hand of the Emperor; and a man whom he decorated with his own hand, you see, could not be so bad a fellow, though he may have had the misfortune to lose his papers - and his purse. That's what has happened to me, and made me so pressing about the damages."

"How and where did you suffer this loss?"

"I do not know, Mr. Burgomaster; I am sure that the evening before last, at bed-time, I took a little money out of the purse, and saw the portfolio in its place; yesterday I had small change sufficient, and did not undo the knapsack."

"And where then has the knapsack been kept?"

"In the room occupied by the children: but this night -"

Dagobert was here interrupted by the tread of some one mounting the stairs: it was the Prophet. Concealed in the shadow of the staircase, he had listened to this conversation, and he dreaded lest the weakness of the burgomaster should mar the complete success of his projects.

CHAPTER XIV

THE DECISION

Morok, who wore his left arm in a sling, having slowly ascended the staircase, saluted the burgomaster respectfully. At sight of the repulsive countenance of the lion-tamer, Rose and Blanche, affrighted, drew back a step nearer to the soldier. The brow of the latter grew dark, for he felt his blood boil against Morok, the cause of all his difficulties - though he was yet ignorant that Goliath, at the instigation of the Prophet, had stolen his portfolio and papers.

"What did you want, Morok?" said the burgomaster, with an air half friendly and half displeased. "I told the landlord that I did not wish to be interrupted."

"I have come to render you a service, Mr. Burgomaster."

"A service?"

"Yes, a great service; or I should not have ventured to disturb you. My conscience reproaches me."

"Your conscience."

"Yes, Mr. Burgomaster, it reproaches me for not having told you all that I had to tell about this man; a false pity led me astray."

"Yell, but what have you to tell?"

Morok approached the judge, and spoke to him for sometime in a low voice.

At first apparently much astonished, the burgomaster became by degrees deeply attentive and anxious; every now and then be allowed some exclamation of surprise or doubt to escape him, whilst he glanced covertly at the group formed by Dagobert and the two young girls. By the expression of his countenance, which grew every moment more unquiet, severe, and searching, it was easy to perceive that the interest which the magistrate had felt for the orphans and for the soldier, was gradually changed, by the secret communications of the Prophet, into a sentiment of distrust and hostility.

Dagobert saw this sudden revolution, and his fears, which had been appeased for an instant, returned with redoubled force; Rose and Blanche, confused, and not understanding the object of this mute scene, looked atthe soldier with increased perplexity.

"The devil!" said the burgomaster, rising abruptly; "all of this never occurred to me. What could I have been thinking of? - But you see, Morok, when one is roused up in the middle of the night, one has not always presence of mind. You said well: it is a great service you came to render me."

"I assert nothing positively, but -"

"No matter; 'tis a thousand to one that you are right."

"It is only a suspicion founded upon divers circumstances; but even a suspicion -"

"May give you scent of the truth. And here was I, going like a gull into the snare! - Once more, what could I have been thinking of?"

"It is so difficult to be on guard against certain appearances."

"You need not tell me so, my dear Morok, you need not tell me so."

During this mysterious conversation, Dagobert was on thorns; he saw vaguely that a violent storm was about to burst. He thought only of how he should still keep his anger within bounds.

Morok again approached the judge, and glancing at the orphans, recommenced speaking in a low voice. "Oh" cried the burgomaster, with, indignation, "you go too far now."

"I affirm nothing," said Morok, hastily; "it is a mere supposition founded on -" and he again brought his lips close to the ear of the judge.

"After all, why not?" resumed the magistrate, lifting up his hands; "such people are capable of anything. He says that he brings them from the heart of Siberia: why may not all this prove to be a tissue of impudent falsehoods? - But I am not to be made a dupe twice," cried the burgomaster, in an angry tone, for, like all persons of a weak and shifting character, he was without pity for those whom he thought capable of having beguiled his compassion.

"Do not be in a hurry to decide - don't give to my words more weight than they deserve," resumed Morok with a hypocritical affectation of humility. "I am unhappily placed in so false a position with regard to this man," - pointing to Dagober - "that I might be thought to have acted from private resentment for the injury he has done me; perhaps I may so act without knowing it, while I fancy that I am only influenced by love of justice, horror of falsehood, and respect for our holy religion. Well - who lives long enough will know - and may heaven forgive me if I am deceived! - In any case, the law will pronounce upon it; and if they should prove innocent, they will be released in a month or two."

"And, for that reason, I need not hesitate. It is a mere measure of precaution; they will not die of it. Besides, the more I think of it, the more it seems probable. Yes this man is doubtless a French spy or agitator, especially when I compare these suspicions with the late demonstration of the students at Frankfort."

"And, upon that theory, nothing is better fitted to excite and stir up those hot-headed youths than -" He glanced significantly at the two sisters; then, after a pause, he added with a sigh, "Satan does not care by what means he works out his ends!"

"Certainly, it would be odious, but well-devised."

"And then, Mr Burgomaster, look at him attentively: you will see that this man has a dangerous face. You will see -"

In continuing thus to speak in a low tone, Morok had evidently pointed to Dagobert. The latter, notwithstanding his self-command, felt that the restraint he had imposed upon himself, since his arrival at this unlucky inn, and above all wince the commencement of the conversation between Morok and the burgomaster, was becoming no longer bearable; besides, he saw clearly that all his efforts to conciliate the favor of the judge were rendered completely null by the fatal influence of the brute-tamer; so, losing patience, he advanced towards him with his arms folded on his breast, and said to him in a subdued voice: "Was it of me that you were whispering to Mr. Burgomaster?"

"Yes," said Morok, looking fixedly at him.

"Why did you not speak out loud?" Having said this, the almost convulsive movement of his thick moustache, as he stood looping Morok full in the face, gave evidence of a severe internal conflict. Seeing that his adversary preserved a contemptuous silence, he repeated in a sterner voice: "I ask you, why you did not speak out loud to Mr. Burgomaster, when you were talking of me?"

"Because there are some things so shameful, that one would blush to utter them aloud," answered Morok insolently.

Till then Dagobert had kept his arms folded; he now extended them violently, clenching his fists. This sudden movement was so expressive that the two sisters uttered a cry of terror, and drew closer to him.

"Hark ye, Mr. Burgomaster!" said the soldier, grinding his teeth with rage: "bid that man go down, or I will not answer for myself!"

"What!" said the burgomaster, haughtily; "do you dare to give orders to me?"

"I tell you to make that man go down," resumed Dagobert, quite beside himself, "or there will be mischief!"

"Dagobert! - good heaven! - be calm," cried the children, grasping his hands.

"It becomes you, certainly - miserable vagabond that you are - not to say worse," returned the burgomaster, in a rage: "it becomes you to give orders to me! - Oh! you think to impose upon me, by telling me you have lost your papers! - It will not serve your turn, for which you carry about with you these two girls, who, in spite of their innocent looks, are perhaps after all -"

"Wretch!" cried Dagobert, with so terrible a voice and gesture that the official did not dare to finish. Taking the children by the arm before they could speak a word, the soldier pushed them back into the chamber; then, locking the door, and putting the key into his pocket, he returned precipitately towards the burgomaster, who, frightened at the menacing air and attitude of the veteran, retreated a couple of steps, and held by one hand to the rail of the staircase.

"Listen to me!" said the soldier, seizing the judge by the arm. "Just now, that scoundrel insulted me - I bore with it - for it only concerned myself. I have heard patiently all your idle talk, because you seemed for a moment to interest yourself in those poor children. But since you have neither soul, nor pity, nor justice - I tell you that, burgomaster though you are - I will spurn you as I would spurn that dog," pointing again to the Prophet, "if you have the misfortune to mention those two young girls, in any other way than you would speak of your own child! - Now, do you mark me?"

"What! - you dare to say," cried the burgomaster, stammering with rage, "that if I happen to mention two adventuresses -"

"Hats off! - when you speak of the daughters of the Duke of Ligny," cried the soldier, snatching the cap of the burgomaster and flinging it on the ground. On this act of aggression, Morok could not restrain his joy. Exasperated and losing all hope, Dagobert had at length yielded to the violence of his anger, after struggling so painfully against it for some hours.

When the burgomaster saw his cap at his feet, he looked at the brute tamer with an air of stupefaction, as if he hesitated to believe so great an enormity. Dagobert, regretting, his violence, and feeling that no means of conciliation note remained, threw a rapid glance around him, and, retreating several paces, gained the topmost steps of the staircase. The burgomaster stood near the bench, in a corner of the landing-place, whilst Morok, with his arm in the sling, to give the more serious appearance to his wound, was close beside him. "So!" cried the magistrate, deceived by the backward movement of Dagobert, "you think to escape, after daring to lift hand against me! - Old villain!"

"Forgive me, Mr. Burgomaster! It was a burst of rashness that I was not able to control. I am sorry for it," said Dagobert in a repentant voice, and hanging his head humbly.

"No pity for thee, rascal! You would begin again to smooth me over with your coaxing ways, but I have penetrated your secret

Eugene Sue

designs. You are not what you appear to be, and there is perhaps an affair of state at the bottom of all this," added the magistrate, in a very diplomatic tone. "All means are alike to those who wish to set Europe in flames."

"I am only a poor devil, Mr. Burgomaster; you, that have a good heart, will show me some mercy."

"What! when you have pulled off my cap?"

"And you," added the soldier, turning towards Morok, "you, that have been the cause of all this - have same pity upon me - do not bear malice! - You, a holy man, speak a word in my favor to Mr. Burgomaster."

"I have spoken to him what I was bound to speak," answered the Prophet ironically.

"Oho! you can look foolish enough now, you old vagabond! Did you think to impose on me with lamentations?" resumed the burgomaster, advancing towards Dagobert. "Thanks be, I am no longer your dupe! - You shall see that we have good dungeons at Leipsic for French agitators and female vagrants, for your damsels are no better than you are. Come," added he, puffing out his cheeks with an important air, "go down before me - and as for you, Morok -"

The burgomaster was unable to finish. For some minutes Dagobert had only sought to gain time, and had cast many a side-glance at a half-open door on the landing-place, just opposite to the chamber occupied by the orphans: finding the moment favorable, he now rushed quick as lightning on the burgomaster, seized him by the throat, and dashed him with such violence against the door in question, that the magistrate, stupefied by this sudden attack, and unable to speak a word or utter a cry, rolled over to the further end of the room, which was completely dark. Then, turning towards Morok, who, with his arm encumbered by the sling, made a rush for the staircase, the soldier caught him by his long, streaming hair, pulled him back, clasped him with hands of iron, clapped his hand over his mouth to stifle his outcries, and notwithstanding his desperate resistance, dragged him into the chamber, on the floor of which the burgomaster lay bruised and stunned.

Having double-locked the door, and put the key in his pocket, Dagobert descended the stairs at two bounds, and found himself in a passage, that opened on the court-yard. The gate of the inn was shut, and there was no possibility of escape on that side. The rain fell in torrents. He could see through the window of a parlor, in which a fire was burning, the host and his people waiting for the decision of the burgomaster. To bolt the door of the passage, and thus intercept all communication with the yard, was for the soldier the affair of an instant, and he hastened upstairs again to rejoin the orphans.

Morok, recovering from his surprise, was calling for help with all his might; but, even if the distance had permitted him to be heard, the noise of the wind and rain would have drowned his outcries. Dagobert had about an hour before him, for it would require some time to elapse before the length of his interview with the magistrate would excite astonishment; and, suspicion or fear once awakened, it would be necessary to break open two doors - that which separated the passage from the court-yard, and that of the room in which the burgomaster and the Prophet were confined.

"My children, it is now time to prove that you have a soldier's blood in your veins," said Dagobert, as he entered abruptly the chamber of the young girls, who were terrified at the racket they had heard for some minutes.

"Good heaven, Dagobert! what has happened?" cried Blanche.

"What do you wish us to do?" added Rose.

Without answering, the soldier ran to the bed, tore off the sheets, tied them strongly together, made a knot at one end, passed it over the top of the left half of the casement, and so shut it in. Thus made fast by the size of the knot, which could not slip through, the sheets, floating on the outside, touched the ground. The second half of the window was left open, to afford a passage to the fugitives.

The veteran next took his knapsack, the children's portmanteau, and the reindeer pelisse, and threw them all out of the window, making a sign to Spoil-sport to follow, to watch over them. The dog did not hesitate, but disappeared at a single bound. Rose and Blanche looked at Dagobert in amazement, without uttering a word.

"Now, children," said he to them, "the doors of the inn are shut, and it is by this way," pointing to the window, "that we must pass - if we would not be arrested, put in prison - you in one place, and I in the other - and have our journey altogether knocked on the head."

"Arrested! put in prison!" cried Rose.

"Separated from you!" exclaimed Blanche.

"Yes, my poor children! - They have killed Jovial - we must make our escape on foot, and try to reach Leipsic - when you are tired, I will carry you, and, though I have to beg my way, we will go through with it. But a quarter of an hour later, and all will be lost. Come, children, have trust in me - show that the daughters of General Simon are no cowards - and there is yet hope."

By a sympathetic movement, the sisters joined hands, as though they would meet the danger united. Their sweet faces, pale from the effect of so many painful emotions, were now expressive of simple resolve, founded on the blind faith they reposed in the devotion of the soldier.

"Be satisfied, Dagobert! we'll not be frightened," said Rose, in a firm voice.

"We will do what must be done," added Blanche, in a no less resolute tone.

"I was sure of it," cried Dagobert; "good blood is ever thicker than water. Come! you are light as feathers, the sheet is strong, it is hardly eight feet to the ground, and the pup is waiting for you."

"It is for me to go first - I am the eldest for to-day," cried Rose, when she had tenderly embraced Blanche; and she ran to the window, in order, if there were any danger, to expose herself to it before her sister.

Dagobert easily guessed the cause of this eagerness. "Dear children!" said he, "I understand you. But fear nothing for one another - there is no danger. I have myself fastened the sheet. Quick, my little Rose!"

As light as a bird, the young girl mounted the ledge of the window, and assisted by Dagobert, took hold of the sheet, and slid gently down according to the recommendation of the soldier, who, leaning out his whole body, encouraged her with his voice.

"Don't be afraid, sister!" said she, as soon as she touched the ground, "it is very easy to come down this way. And Spoil-sport is here, licking my hands." Blanche did not long keep her waiting; as courageous as her sister, she descended with the same success.

"Dear little creatures! what have they done to be so unfortunate? - Thousand thunders! there must be a curse upon the family," cried Dagobert, as, with heavy heart, he saw the pale, sweet face of the young girl disappear amid the gloom of the dark night, which violent squalls of wind and torrents of rain rendered still more dismal.

"Dagobert, we are waiting for you; come quickly!" said the orphans in a low voice, from beneath the window. Thanks to his tall stature, the soldier rather leaped than glided to the ground.

Dagobert and the two young girls had not fled from the inn of the White Falcon more than a quarter of an hour, when a long crash resounded through the house. The door had yielded to the efforts of the burgomaster and Morok, who had made use of a heavy table as a battering ram. Guided by the light, they ran to the chamber of the orphans, now deserted. Morok saw the sheets floating from the casement, and cried: "Mr. Burgomaster, they have escaped by the window - they are on foot - in this dark and stormy night, they cannot be far."

"No doubt, we shall catch them, the miserable tramps! Oh, I will be revenged! Quick, Morok; your honor is concerned as well as mine."

"My honor? - Much more is concerned than that, Mr. Burgomaster," answered the Prophet, in a tone of great irritation. Then, rapidly descending the stairs, he opened the door of the court-yard, and shouted in a voice of thunder:

"Goliath! unchain the dogs! - and, landlord! bring us lanterns, torches - arm your people - open the doors! - We must pursue the fugitives; they cannot escape us; we must have them - alive or dead!"

CHAPTER XV

THE DESPATCHES

When we read, in the rules of the order of the Jesuits, under the title De formula scribendi (Institut. 2, 11, p. 125, 129), the development of the 8th part of the constitutions, we are appalled by the number of letters, narratives, registers, and writings of all kinds, preserved in the archives of the society.

It is a police infinitely more exact and better informed than has ever been that of any state. Even the government of Venice found itself surpassed by the Jesuits: when it drove them out in 1606, it seized all their papers, and reproached them for their great and laborious curiosity. This police, this secret inquisition, carried to such a degree of perfection, may give some idea of the strength of a government, so well-informed so persevering in its projects, so powerful by its unity, and, as the constitutions have it, by the union of its members. It is not hard to understand, what immense force must belong to the heads of this society, and how the general of the Jesuits could say to the Duke de Brissac: "From this room, your grace, I govern not only Paris, but China - not only China, but the whole world - and all without any one knowing how it is done:" (Constitution of the Jesuits, edited by Paulin, Paris, 1843.)

Morok, the lion-tamer, seeing Dagobert deprived of his horse, and stripped of his money and papers, and thinking it was thus out of his power to continue his journey, had, previous to the arrival of the burgomaster, despatched Karl to Leipsic, as the bearer of a letter which he was to put immediately into the post. The address of this letter was as follows: "A Monsieur Rodin, Rue du Milieu des Ursins, Paris."

About the middle of this obscure and solitary street, situate below the level of the Quai Napoleon, which it joins not far from the Rue Saint Landry, there stood a house of unpretentious appearance, at the bottom of a dark and narrow court-yard, separated from the street by a low building in front, with arched doorway, and two windows protected by thick iron bars. Nothing could be more simple than the interior of this quiet dwelling, as was sufficiently shown by the furniture of a pretty large room on the ground floor. The walls of this apartment were lined with old gray wainscot; the tiled floor was painted red, and carefully polished; curtains of white calico shaded the windows.

A sphere of about four feet in diameter, raised on a pedestal of massive oak, stood at one end of the room, opposite to the fireplace. Upon this globe, which was painted on a large scale, a host of little red crosses appeared scattered over all parts of the world - from the North to the South, from the rising to the setting sun, from the most barbarous countries, from the most distant isles, to the centres of civilization, to France itself. There was not a single country which did not present some spots marked with these red crosses, evidently indicative of stations, or serving as points of reference.

Before a table of black wood, loaded with papers, and resting against the wall near the chimney, a chair stood empty. Further on, between the two windows, was a large walnut-wood desk, surmounted by shelves full of pasteboard boxes.

At the end of the month of October, 1831, about eight o'clock in the morning, a man sat writing at this desk. This was M. Rodin, the correspondent of Morok, the brute-tamer.

About fifty years of age, he wore an old, shabby, olive

greatcoat, with a greasy collar, a snuff-powdered cotton handkerchief for a cravat, and waistcoat and trousers of threadbare black cloth. His feet, buried in loose varnished shoes, rested on a petty piece of green baize upon the red, polished floor. His gray hair lay flat on his temples, and encircled his bald forehead; his eyebrows were scarcely marked; his upper eyelid, flabby and overhanging, like the membrane which shades the eyes of reptiles, half concealed his small, sharp, black eye. His thin lips, absolutely colorless, were hardly distinguishable from the wan hue of his lean visage, with its pointed nose and chin; and this livid mask (deprived as it were of lips) appeared only the more singular, from its maintaining a death-like immobility. Had it not been for the rapid movement of his fingers, as, bending over the desk, he scratched along with his pen, M. Rodin might have been mistaken for a corpse.

By the aid of a cipher (or secret alphabet) placed before him he was copying certain passages from a long sheet full of writing, in a manner quite unintelligible to those who did not possess the key to the system. Whilst the darkness of the day increased the gloom of the large, cold, naked-looking apartment, there was something awful in the chilling aspect of this man, tracing his mysterious characters in the midst of profound silence.

The clock struck eight. The dull sound of the knocker at the outer door was heard, then a bell tinkled twice, several doors opened and shut, and a new personage entered the chamber. On seeing him, M. Rodin rose from the desk, stuck his pen between his teeth, bowed with a deeply submissive air, and sat down again to his work without uttering a word.

The two formed a striking contrast to one another. The newcomer, though really older than he seemed, would have passed for thirty-six or thirty eight years of age at most. His figure was tall and shapely, and few could have encountered the brightness of his large gray eye, brilliant as polished steel. His nose, broad at the commencement, formed a well-cut square at its termination; his chin was prominent, and the bluish tints of his close-shaved beard were contrasted with the bright carnation of his lips, and the whiteness of his fine teeth. When he took off his hat to change it for a black velvet cap which he found on the small table, he displayed a quantity of light chestnut hair, not yet silvered by time. He was dressed in a long frock-coat, buttoned up to the neck in military fashion.

The piercing glance and broad forehead of this man revealed a powerful intellect, even as the development of his chest and shoulders announced a vigorous physical organization; whilst his gentlemanly appearance, the perfection of his gloves and boots, the light perfume which hung about his hair and person, the grace and ease of his least movements, betrayed what is called the man of the world, and left the impression that he had sought or might still seek every kind of success, from the most frivolous to the most serious. This rare combination of strength of mind, strength of body, and extreme elegance of manners, was in this instance rendered still more striking by the circumstance, that whatever there might be of haughtiness or command in the upper part of that energetic countenance, was softened down, and tempered by a constant but not uniform smile - for, as occasion served, this smile became either kind or sly, cordial or gay, discreet or prepossessing, and thus augmented the insinuating charm of this man, who, once seen, was never again forgotten. But, in yielding to this involuntary sympathy, the doubt occurred if the influence was for good - or for evil.

M. Rodin, the secretary of the newcomer, continued to write.

"Are there any letters from Dunkirk, Rodin?" inquired his master.

"Post not yet in."

"Without being positively uneasy as to my mother's health, since she was already convalescent," resumed the other, "I shall only be quite reassured by a letter from my excellent friend, the Princess de Saint Dizier. I shall have good news this morning,

I hope."

"It is to be desired," said the secretary, as humble and submissive as he was laconic and impassible.

"Certainly it is to be desired," resumed his master; "for one of the brightest days of my life was when the Princess de Saint-Dizier announced to me that this sudden and dangerous illness had yielded to the care and attention with which she surrounds my mother. Had it not been for that I must have gone down to her instantly, though my presence here is very necessary."

Then, approaching the desk, he added: "Is the summary of the foreign correspondence complete?"

"Here is the analysis."

"The letters are still sent under envelope to the places named, and are then brought here as I directed?"

"Always."

"Read to me the notes of this correspondence; if there are any letters for me to answer, I will tell you." And Rodin's master began to walk up and down the room, with his hands crossed behind his back, dictating observations of which Rodin took careful note.

The secretary turned to a pretty large pile of papers, and thus began:

"Don Raymond Olivarez acknowledges from Cadiz receipt of letter No.19; he will conform to it, and deny all share in the abduction."

"Very well; file it."

"Count Romanoff, of Riga, finds himself in a position of pecuniary embarrassment."

"Let Duplessis send him fifty louis; I formerly served as captain in his regiment, and he has since given us good information."

"They have received at Philadelphia the last cargo of Histories of France, expurgated for the use of the faithful they require some more of the same sort."

"Take note of it, and write to Duplessis. Go on."

"M. Spindler sends from Namur the secret report on M. Ardouin."

"To be examined."

"M. Ardouin sends from the same town the secret report on M. Spindler."

"To be examined."

"Doctor Van Ostadt, of the same town, sends a confidential note on the subject of Messrs. Spindler and Ardouin."

"To be compared. Go on!"

"Count Malipierri, of Turin, announces that the donation of 300,000 francs is signed."

"Inform Duplessis. What next?"

"Don Stanislaus has just quitted the waters of Baden with Queen Marie Ernestine. He informs us that her majesty will receive with gratitude the promised advices, and will answer them with her own hand."

"Make a note of it. I will myself write to the queen."

Whilst Rodin was inscribing a few remarks on the margin of the paper, his master, continuing to walk up and down the room, found himself opposite to the globe marked with little red crosses, and stood contemplating it for a moment with a pensive air.

Rodin continued: "In consequence of the state of the public mind in certain parts of Italy, where sundry agitators have turned their eyes in the direction of France, Father Arsenio writes from Milan, that it would be of importance to distribute profusely in that country, some little book, in which the French would be represented as impious and debauched, rapacious and bloody."

"The idea is excellent. We might turn to good account the excesses committed by our troops in Italy during the wars of the Republic. You must employ Jacques Dumoulin to write it. He is full of gall, spite, and venom: the pamphlet will be scorching. Besides, I may furnish a few notes; but you must not pay Dumoulin till after delivery of the manuscript."

"That is well understood: for, if we were to pay him beforehand, he would be drunk for a week in some low den. It was thus we had to pay him twice over for his virulent attack on the pantheistic tendencies of Professor Martin's philosophy."

"Take note of it - and go on!"

"The merchant announces that the clerk is about to send the banker to give in his accounts. You understand?' added Rodin, after pronouncing these words with a marked emphasis.

"Perfectly," said the other, with a start; "they are but the expressions agreed on. What next?"

"But the clerk," continued the secretary, "is restrained by a last scruple."

After a moment's silence, during which the features of Rodin's master worked strongly, he thus resumed: "They must continue to act on the clerk's mind by silence and solitude;

then, let him read once more the list of cases in which regicide is authorized and absolved. Go on!"

"The woman Sydney writes from Dresden, that she waits for instructions. Violent scenes of jealousy on her account have again taken place between the father and son; but neither from these new bursts of mutual hatred, nor from the confidential communications which each has made to her against his rival, has she yet been able to glean the information required. Hitherto, she has avoided giving the preference to one or the other; but, should this situation be prolonged, she fears it may rouse their suspicion. Which ought she then to choose - the father or the son?"

"The son - for jealous resentment will be much more violent and cruel in the old man, and, to revenge himself for the preference bestowed upon his son, he will perhaps tell what they have both such an interest to conceal. The next?"

"Within the last three years, two maid-servants of Ambrosius whom we placed in that little parish in the mountains of the Valais, have disappeared, without any one knowing what has become of them. A third has just met with the same fate. The Protestants of the country are roused - talk of murder with frightful attendant circumstances -"

"Until there is proof positive and complete of the fact, Ambrosius must be defended against these infamous calumnies, the work of a party that never shrinks from; monstrous inventions. Go on!"

"Thompson, of Liverpool, has at length succeeded in procuring for Justin the place of agent or manager to Lord Stewart, a rich Irish Catholic, whose head grows daily weaker."

"Let the fact be once verified, and Thompson shall have a premium of fifty louis. Make a note of it for Duplessis. Proceed."

"Frantz Dichstein, of Vienna," resumed Rodin, "announces that his father has just died of the cholera, in a little village at some leagues from that city: for the epidemic continues to advance slowly, coming from the north of Russia by way of Poland."

"It is true," said Rodin's master, interrupting him; "may its terrible march be stayed, and France be spared."

"Frantz Dichstein," resumed Rodin, "says that his two brothers are determined to contest the donation made by his father, but that he is of an opposite opinion."

"Consult the two persons that are charged with all matters of litigation. What next?"

"The Cardinal Prince d'Amalfi will conform to the three first points of the proposal: he demands to make a reservation upon the fourth point."

"No reserve! - Either full and absolute acceptance - or else war - and (mark me well) war without mercy - on him and his creatures. Go on!"

"Fra Paolo announces that the Prince Boccari, chief of a redoubtable secret society, in despair at seeing his friends accuse him of treachery, in consequence of suspicions excited in their minds by Fra Paolo himself, has committed suicide."

"Boccari! is it possible?" cried Rodin's master. "Boccari! the patriot Boccari! so dangerous a person!"

"The patriot Boccari," repeated the impassible secretary.

"Tell Duplessis to send an order for five-and-twenty louis to Fra Paolo. Make a note of it."

"Hausman informs us that the French dancer, Albertine Ducornet, is the mistress of the reigning prince; she has the most complete influence over him, and it would be easy through her means to arrive at the end proposed, but that she is herself governed by her lover (condemned in France as a forger), and that she does nothing without consulting him."

"Let Hausman get hold of this man - if his claims are reasonable, accede to them - and learn if the girl has any relations in Paris."

"The Duke d'Orbano announces, that the king his master will authorize the new establishment, but on the conditions previously stated."

"No condition! - either a frank adhesion or a positive refusal. Let us know our friends from our enemies. The more unfavorable the circumstances, the more we must show firmness, and overbear opposition by confidence in ourselves."

"The same also announces, that the whole of the corps diplomatique continues to support the claims of the father of that young Protestant girl, who refuses to quit the convent where she has taken refuge, unless it be to marry her lover against her father's will."

"Ah! the corps diplomatique continues to remonstrate in the father's name?"

"Yes."

"Then, continue to answer, that the spiritual power has nothing to do with the temporal."

At this moment, the bell of the outer door again sounded twice. "See who it is," said Rodin's master; and the secretary rose and left the room. The other continued to walk thoughtfully up and down, till, coming near to the huge globe, he stopped short before it.

For some time he contemplated, in profound silence, the

innumerable little red crosses, which appeared to cover, as with an immense net, all the countries of the earth. Reflecting doubtless on the invisible action of his power, which seemed to extend over the whole world, the features of this man became animated, his large gray eye sparkled, his nostrils swelled, and his manly countenance assumed an indescribable expression of pride, energy, and daring. With haughty brow and scornful lip, he drew still nearer to the globe, and leaned his strong hand upon the pole.

This powerful pressure, an imperious movement, as of one taking possession, seemed to indicate, that he felt sure of governing this globe, on which he looked down from the height of his tall figure, and on which he rested his hand with so lofty and audacious an air of sovereignty.

But now he no longer smiled. His eye threatened, and his large forehead was clad with a formidable scowl. The artist, who had wished to paint the demon of craft and pride, the infernal genius of insatiable domination, could not have chosen a more suitable model.

When Rodin returned, the face of his master had recovered its ordinary expression. "It is the postman," said Rodin, showing the letters which he held in his hand; "there is nothing from Dunkirk."

"Nothing?" cried his master - and his painful emotion formed a strange contrast to his late haughty and implacable expression of countenance - "nothing? no news of my mother? - Thirty-six hours more, then, of anxiety."

"It seems to me, that, if the princess had bad news to give, she would have written. Probably the improvement goes on."

"You are doubtless right, Rodin - but no matter - I am far from easy. If, to-morrow, the news should not be completely satisfactory, I set out for the estate of the princess. Why would my mother pass the autumn in that part of the country? The environs of Dunkirk do not, I fear, agree with her."

After a few moments' silence, he added, as he continued to walk: "Well - these letters - whence are they?"

Rodin looked at the post-marks, and replied: "Out of the four there are three relative to the great and important affairs of the medals."

"Thank heaven! - provided the news be favorable," cried his master, with an expression of uneasiness, which showed how much importance he attached to this affair.

"One is from Charlestown, and no doubt relative to Gabriel, the missionary," answered Rodin; "this other from Batavia, and no doubt concerns the Indian, Djalma. The third is from Leipsic, and will probably confirm that received yesterday, in which the lion-tamer, Morok, informed us, that, in accordance with his orders, and without his being compromised in any way, the daughters of General Simon would not be able to continue their journey."

At the name of General Simon, a cloud passed over the features of Rodin's master.

CHAPTER XVI

THE ORDERS

The principal houses correspond with that in Paris; they are also in direct communication with the General, who resides at Rome. The correspondence of the Jesuits so active, various, and organized in so wonderful a manner, has for its object to supply the heads with all the information they can require. Every day, the General receives a host of reports, which serve to check one another. In the central house, at Rome, are immense registers, in which are inscribed the names of all the Jesuits, of their adherents, and of all the considerable persons, whether friends or enemies, with whom they have any connection. In these registers are reported, without alteration, hatred or passion the facts relating to the life of each individual. It is the most gigantic biographical collection that has ever been formed. The frailties of a woman, the secret errors of a statesman, are chronicled in this book with the same cold impartiality. Drawn up for the purpose of being useful, these biographies are necessarily exact. When the Jesuits wish to influence an individual, they have but to turn to this book, and they know immediately his life, his character, his parts, his faults, his projects, his family, his friends, his most sacred ties. Conceive, what a superior facility of action this immense police-register, which includes the whole world, must give to any one society! It is not lightly that I speak of these registers; I have my facts from a person who has seen this collection, and who is perfectly well acquainted with the Jesuits. Here then, is matter to reflect on for all those families, who admit freely into

Eugene Sue

their houses the members of a community that carries its biographical researches to such a point. (Libri, Member of the Institute. Letters on the Clergy.)

When he had conquered the involuntary emotion which the name or remembrance of General Simon had occasioned, Rodin's master said to the secretary: "Do not yet open the letters from Leipsic, Charlestown, and Batavia; the information they contain will doubtless find its place presently. It will save our going over the same ground twice."

The secretary looked inquiringly at his master.

The latter continued - "Have you finished the note relating to the medals?"

"Here it is," replied the secretary; "I was just finishing my interpretation of the cipher."

"Read it to me, in the order of the facts. You can append to it the news contained in those three letters."

"True," said Rodin; "in that way the letters will find their right place."

"I wish to see," rejoined the other, "whether this note is clear and fully explanatory; you did not forget that the person it is intended for ought not to know all?"

"I bore it in mind, and drew up the paper accordingly."

"Read," said the master.

M. Rodin read as follows, slowly and deliberately:

"'A hundred and fifty years ago, a French Protestant family, foreseeing the speedy - revocation of the edict of Nantes, went into voluntary exile, in order to avoid the just and rigorous decrees already issued against the members of the reformed church - those indomitable foes of our holy religion.

"'Some members of this family sought refuge in Holland, and afterwards in the Dutch colonies; others in Poland, others in Germany; some in England, and some in America.

"'It is supposed that only seven descendants remain of this family, which underwent strange vicissitudes since; its present representatives are found in all ranks of society, from the sovereign to the mechanic.

"'These descendants, direct or indirect, are:

"'On the mother's side,

"'Rose and Blanche Simon - minors.

"'General Simon married, at Warsaw, a descendant of the said family.

"'Francois Hardy, manufacturer at Plessis, near Paris.

"'Prince Djalma, son of Kadja-sing, King of Mondi.

"'Kadja-sing, married, in 1802, a descendant of the said family, then settled at Batavia, in the Island of Java, a Dutch colony.

"'On the father's side - Jacques Rennepont, surnamed Sleepinbuff, mechanic.

"'Adrienne de Cardoville, daughter of the Count of Rennepont, Duke of Cardoville.

"'Gabriel Rennepont, priest of the foreign missions.

"'All the members of this family possess, or should possess, a bronze medal bearing the following inscriptions:

Victim

of
L. C. D. J.
Pray for me!
Paris
February the 13th, 1682.

At Paris,
Rue Saint Francois, No. 3,
In a century and a half
you will be.
February the 13th, 1832.
Pray For Me!

"'These words and dates show that all of them have a great interest to be at Paris on the 13th of February, 1832; and that, not by proxy, but in person, whether they are minors, married or single.

"'But other persons have an immense interest that none of the descendants of this family be at Paris on the 13th February, except Gabriel Rennepont, priest of the foreign missions.

"'At all hazards, therefore, Gabriel must be the only person present at the appointment made with the descendants of this family, a century and a half ago.

"'To prevent the other six persons from reaching Paris on the said day, or to render their presence of no effect, much has been already done; but much remains to be done to ensure the success of this affair, which is considered as the most vital and most important of the age, on account of its probable results.'"

"'Tis but too true," observed Rodin's master, interrupting him, and shaking his head pensively. "And, moreover, that the consequences of success are incalculable, and there is no forseeing what may follow failure. In a word, it almost involves a question of existence or non existence during several years. To succeed, therefore, 'all possible means must be employed. Nothing must be shunned,' except, however, that appearances must be skillfully maintained."

"I have written it," said Rodin, having added the words his master had just dictated, who then said,

"Continue."

Rodin read on:

"'To forward or secure the affair in question, it is necessary to give some private and secret particulars respecting the seven persons who represent this family.

"'The truth of these particulars may be relied on. In case of need they might be completed in the most minute degree for contradictory information having been given, very lengthened evidence has been obtained. The order in which the names of the persons stand will be observed, and events that have happened up to the present time will only be mentioned.

"'NOTE, No. I.

"'Rose and Blanche Simon, twin sisters, about fifteen years of age; very pretty, so much alike, one might be taken for the other; mild and timid disposition, but capable of enthusiasm. Brought up in Siberia by their mother, a woman of strong mind and deistical sentiments, they are wholly ignorant of our holy religion.

"'General Simon, separated from his wife before they were born, is not aware, even now, that he has two daughters.

"'It was hoped that their presence in Paris, on the 13th of February, would be prevented, by sending their mother to a place of exile, much more distant than the one first allotted her; but their mother dying, the Governor of Siberia, who is wholly ours, supposing, by a deplorable mistake, that the measure only affected the wife of General Simon personally, unfortunately allowed the girls to return to France, under the guidance of an old soldier.

"'This man is enterprising, faithful, and determined. He is noted down as dangerous.

"'The Simon girls are inoffensive. It is hoped, on fair grounds, that they are now detained in the neighborhood of Leipsic.'"

Rodin's master interrupted him, saying:

"Now, read the letter just received from Leipsic; it may complete the information."

Rodin read it, and exclaimed:

"Excellent news! The maidens and their guide had succeeded in escaping during the night from the White Falcon Tavern, but all three were overtaken and seized about a league from Mockern. They have been transferred to Leipsic, where they are imprisoned as vagabonds; their guide, the soldier, is accused and condemned of resisting the authorities, and using violence to a magistrate."

"It is almost certain, then, considering the tedious mode of proceeding in Germany (otherwise we would see to it), that the girls will not be able to be here on the 13th February," added Rodin's master. "Append this to the note on the back."

The secretary obeyed, and endorsed "An abstract of Morok's letter."

"It is written," he then added.

"Go on," resumed his master.

Rodin continued reading.

"'NOTE, No. II.

"'Francois Hardy, manufacturer at Plessis, near Paris, forty years old; a steady, rich, intelligent, active, honest, well-informed man, idolized by his workmen - thanks to numberless innovations to promote their welfare. Never attending to the duties of our holy religion. Noted down as a very dangerous man: but the hatred and envy he excites among other manufacturers, especially in M. le Baron Tripeaud, his competitor, may easily be turned against him. If other means of action on his account, and against him, are necessary, the evidence may be consulted; it is very voluminous. This man has been marked and watched for a long time.

"'He has been so effectually misguided with respect to the medal, that he is completely deceived as to the interests it represents. He is, however, constantly watched, surrounded, and governed, without suspecting it; one of his dearest friends deceives him, and through his means we know his secret thoughts.

"'NOTE, No. III.

"'Prince Djalma; eighteen; energetic and generous, haughty, independent and wild; favorite of General Simon, who commanded the troops of his father, Kadja-sing, in the struggle maintained by the latter against the English in India. Djalma is mentioned only by way of reminder, for his mother died young, while her parents were living. They resided at Batavia. On the death of the latter, neither Djalma nor the king, his father, claimed their little property. It is, therefore, certain that they are ignorant of the grave interests connected with the possession of the medal in question, which formed part of the property of Djalma's mother."

Rodin's master interrupted him.

"Now read the letter from Batavia, and complete the information respecting Djalma."

Rodin read, and then observed:

"Good news again. Joshua Van Dael, merchant at Batavia (he was educated in our Pondicherry establishment), learns from his correspondent at Calcutta that the old Indian king was killed in the last battle with the English. His son, Djalma, deprived of the paternal throne, is provisionally detained as a prisoner of state in an Indian fortress."

"We are at the end of October," said Rodin's master. "If Prince Djalma were to leave India now, he could scarcely reach Paris by the month of February."

"Van Dael," continued Rodin, "regrets that he has not been able to prove his zeal in this case. Supposing Prince Djalma set at liberty, or having effected his escape, it is certain he would come to Batavia to claim his inheritance from his mother, since he has nothing else left him in the world. In that case, you may rely on Van Dael's devotedness. In return, he solicits very precise information, by the next post, respecting the fortune of M. le Baron Tripeaud, banker and manufacturer, with whom he has business transactions."

"Answer that point evasively. Van Dael as yet has only shown zeal; complete the information respecting Djalma from these new tidings."

Rodin wrote.

But in a few minutes his master said to him with a singular expression:

"Does not Van Dael mention General Simon in connection with Djalma's imprisonment and his father's death?"

"He does not allude to him," said the secretary, continuing his task.

Rodin's master was silent, and paced the room.

In a few moments Rodin said to him: "I have done it."

"Go on, then."

"'NOTE, No. IV.

"'Jacques Rennepont, surnamed "Sleepinbuff," i.e. Lie naked, workman in Baron Tripeaud's factory. This artisan is drunken, idle, noisy, and prodigal; he is not without sense, but idleness and debauch have ruined him. A clever agent, on whom we rely, has become acquainted with his mistress, Cephyse Soliveau, nicknamed the Bacchanal Queen. Through her means, the agent has formed such ties with him that he may even now be considered beyond the reach of the interests that ought to insure his presence in Paris on the 13th of February.

"'NOTE, No. V.

"'Gabriel Rennepont, priest of foreign missions, distant relation of the above, but he is alike ignorant of the existence of his relative and the relationship. An orphan foundling, he was adopted by Frances Baudoin, the wife of a soldier going by the name Dagobert.

"'Should this soldier, contrary to expectation, reach Paris, his wife would be a powerful means of influencing him. She is an excellent creature, ignorant and credulous, of exemplary piety, over whom we have long had unlimited control. She prevailed on Gabriel to take orders, notwithstanding his repugnance.

"'Gabriel is five-and-twenty; disposition as angelic as his countenance; rare and solid virtues; unfortunately he was brought up with his adopted brother, Agricola, Dagobert's son. This Agricola is a poet and workman - but an excellent workman; he is employed by M. Hardy; has imbibed the most detestable doctrines; fond of his mother; honest, laborious, but without religious feeling. Marked as very dangerous. This causes his intimacy with Gabriel to be feared.

"'The latter, notwithstanding his excellent qualities, sometimes causes uneasiness. We have even delayed confiding in him fully. A false step might make him, too, one of the most dangerous. Much precaution must be used then, especially till the 13th of February; since, we repeat it, on him, on his presence in Paris at that time, depend immense hopes and equally important interests.

"'Among other precautions, we have consented to his taking part in the American mission, for he unites with angelic sweetness of character a calm intrepidity and adventurous spirit which could only be satisfied by allowing him to engage in the perilous existence of the missionaries. Luckily, his superiors at Charlestown have received the strictest orders not to endanger, on any account, so precious a life. They are to send him to Paris, at least a month or two before February 13th."'

Rodin's master again interrupted him, and said: "Read the letter from Charlestown, and see what it tells you in order to complete the information upon this point also."

When he had read the letter, Rodin went on: "Gabriel is expected every day from the Rocky Mountains, whither he had absolutely insisted on going alone upon a mission."

"What imprudence!"

"He has no doubt escaped all danger, as he himself announces his speedy return to Charlestown. As soon as he arrives, which cannot (they write) be later than the middle of this month, he will be shipped off for France."

"Add this to the note which concerns him," said Rodin's master.

"It is written," replied the secretary, a few moments later.

"Proceed, then," said his master. Rodin continued

"'NOTE, No. VI.
"'ADRIENNE RENNEPONT DE CARDOVILLE.

"'Distantly related (without knowing it) to Jacques Rennepont, alias Sleepinbuff, and Gabriel Rennepont, missionary priest. She will soon be twenty-one years of age, the most attractive person in the world - extraordinary beauty, though red-haired - a mind remarkable for its originality - immense fortune - all the animal instincts. The incredible independence of her character makes one tremble for the future fate of this young person. Happily, her appointed guardian, Baron Tripeaud (a baron of 1829 creation, formerly agent to the late Count of Rennepont, Duke of Cardoville), is quite in the interest, and almost in the dependence, of the young lady's aunt. We count, with reason, upon this worthy and respectable relative, and on the Baron Tripeaud, to oppose and repress the singular, unheard-of designs which this young person, as resolute as independent, does not fear to avow - and which, unfortunately, cannot be turned to account in the interest of the affair in question - for -"

Rodin was here interrupted by two discreet taps at the door. The secretary rose, went to see who knocked, remained a moment without, and then returned with two letters in his hand, saying: "The princess has profited by the departure of a courier to - "

"Give me the letter!" cried his master, without leaving him time to finish. "At length," he added, "I shall have news of my mother -"

He had scarcely read the first few lines of the letter, when he grew deadly pale, and his features took an expression of painful astonishment and poignant grief. "My mother!" he cried, "oh, heavens! my mother!"

"What misfortune has happened!" asked Rodin, with a look of alarm, as he rose at the exclamation of his master.

"The symptoms of improvement were fallacious," replied the other, dejectedly; "she has now relapsed into a nearly hopeless state. And yet the doctor thinks my presence might save her, for she calls for me without ceasing. She wishes to see me for the last time, that she may die in peace. Oh, that wish is sacred! Not to grant it would be matricide. If I can but arrive in time! Travelling day and night, it will take nearly two days."

"Alas! what a misfortune!" said Rodin, wringing his hands, and raising his eyes to heaven.

His master rang the bell violently, and said to the old servant that opened the door: "Just put what is indispensable into the portmanteau of my travelling-carriage. Let the porter take a cab, and go for post horses instantly. Within an hour, I must be on the road. Mother! mother!" cried he, as the servant departed in haste. "Not to see her again - oh, it would be frightful!" And sinking upon a chair, overwhelmed with sorrow, he covered his face with his hands.

This great grief was sincere - he loved tenderly his mother that divine sentiment had accompanied him, unalterable and pure, through all the phases of a too often guilty life.

After a few minutes, Rodin ventured to say to his master, as he showed him the second letter: "This, also, has just been brought from M. Duplessis. It is very important - very pressing -"

"See what it is, and answer it. I have no head for business."

"The letter is confidential," said Rodin, presenting it to his master. "I dare not open it, as you may see by the mark on the cover."

At sight of this mark, the countenance of Rodin's master assumed an indefinable expression of respect and fear. With a trembling hand he broke the seal. The note contained only the following words: "Leave all business, and without losing a minute, set out and come. M. Duplessis will replace you. He has orders."

"Great God!" cried this man in despair. "Set out before I have seen my mother! It is frightful, impossible - it would perhaps kill her - yes, it would be matricide!"

Whilst he uttered these words, his eyes rested on the huge globe, marked with red crosses. A sudden revolution seemed to take place within him; he appeared to repent of the violence of his regrets; his face, though still sad, became once more calm and grave. He handed the fatal letter to his secretary, and said to him, whilst he stifled a sigh: "To be classed under its proper number."

Rodin took the letter, wrote a number upon it, and placed it in a particular box. After a moment's silence, his master resumed: "You will take orders from M. Duplessis, and work with him. You will deliver to him the note on the affair of the medals; he knows to whom to address it. You will write to Batavia, Leipsic, and Charlestown, in the sense agreed. Prevent, at any price, the daughters of General Simon from quitting Leipsic; hasten the arrival of Gabriel in Paris; and should Prince Djalma come to Batavia, tell M. Joshua Van Dael, that we count on his zeal and obedience to keep him there."

And this man, who, while his dying mother called to him in vain, could thus preserve his presence of mind, entered his own apartments; whilst Rodin busied himself with the answers he had been ordered to write, and transcribed them in cipher.

In about three quarters of an hour, the bells of the post-horses were heard jingling without. The old servant again entered, after discreetly knocking at the door, and said:

"The carriage is ready."

Rodin nodded, and the servant withdrew. The secretary, in his turn, went to knock at the door of the inner room. His master appeared, still grave and cold, but fearfully pale, and holding a letter in his hand.

"This for my mother," said he to Rodin; "you will send a courier on the instant."

"On the instant," replied the secretary.

"Let the three letters for Leipsic, Batavia and Charlestown, leave to-day by the ordinary channel. They are of the last importance. You know it."

Those were his last words. Executing merciless orders with a merciless obedience, he departed without even attempting to see his mother. His secretary accompanied him respectfully to his carriage.

"What road, sir?" asked the postilion, turning round on his saddle.

"The road to ITALY!" answered Rodin's master, with so deep a sigh that it almost resembled a sob.

As the horses started at full gallop, Rodin made a low bow; then he returned to the large, cold, bare apartment. The attitude, countenance, and gait of this personage seemed to have undergone a sudden change. He appeared to have increased in dimensions. He was no longer an automaton, moved by the mechanism of humble obedience. His features, till now impassible, his glance, hitherto subdued, became suddenly animated with an expression of diabolical craft; a sardonic smile curled his thin, pale lips, and a look of grim satisfaction relaxed his cadaverous face.

In turn, he stopped before the huge globe. In turn, he contemplated it in silence, even as his master had done. Then, bending over it, and embracing it, as it were, in his arms, he gloated with his reptile-eye on it for some moments, drew his coarse finger along its polished surface, and tapped his flat, dirty nail on three of the places dotted with red crosses. And, whilst he thus pointed to three towns, in very different parts of the world, he named them aloud, with a sneer.

"Leipsic - Charlestown - Batavia."

"In each of these three places," he added, "distant as they are
from one another, there exist persons who little think that
here, in this obscure street, from the recesses of this chamber,
wakeful eyes are upon them - that all their movements are
followed, all their actions known - and that hence will issue
new instructions, which deeply concern them, and which will
be inexorably executed; for an interest is at stake, which may
have a powerful influence on Europe - on the world. Luckily,
we have friends at Leipsic, Charlestown, and Batavia."

This funny, old, sordid, ill-dressed man, with his livid and
death-like countenance, thus crawling over the sphere before
him, appeared still more awful than his master, when the
latter, erect and haughty, had imperiously laid his hand upon
that globe, which he seemed desirous of subjecting by the
strength of his pride and courage. The one resembled the eagle,
that hovers above his prey - the other the reptile, that envelops
its victim in its inextricable folds.

After some minutes, Rodin approached his desk, rubbing his
hands briskly together, and wrote the following epistle in a
cipher unknown even to his master:

"Paris, 3/4 past 9 A.M.

"He is gone - but he hesitated!

"When he received the order, his dying mother had just
summoned him to her. He might, they told him, save her by
his presence; and he exclaimed: 'Not to go to my mother
would be matricide!'

"Still, he is gone - but he hesitated. I keep my eye upon him
continually. These lines will reach Rome at the same time as
himself.

"P.S. - Tell the Cardinal-Prince that he may rely on me, but I hope for his active aid in return."

When he had folded and sealed this letter, Rodin put it into his pocket. The clock struck ten, M. Rodin's hour for breakfast. He arranged and locked up his papers in a drawer, of which he carried away the key, brushed his old greasy hat with his sleeve, took a patched umbrella in his hand, and went out. [1]

Whilst these two men, in the depths of their obscure retreat, were thus framing a plot, which was to involve the seven descendants of a race formerly proscribed - a strange mysterious defender was planning how to protect this family, which was also his own.

1 Having cited the excellent, courageous letters of M. Libri, and the curious work edited by M. Paulin, it is our duty likewise to mention many bold and conscientious writings on the subject of the "Society of Jesus," recently published by the elder Dupin, Michelet, Quinet, Genin, and the Count de Saint Priest - works of high and impartial intellects, in which the fatal theories of the order are admirably exposed and condemned. We esteem ourselves happy, if we can bring one stone towards the erection of the strong, and, we hope, durable embankment which these generous hearts and noble minds are raising against the encroachments of an impure and always menacing flood. - E. S.

Choose from Thousands of 1stWorldLibrary Classics By

A. M. Barnard
Ada Leverson
Adolphus William Ward
Aesop
Agatha Christie
Alexander Aaronsohn
Alexander Kielland
Alexandre Dumas
Alfred Gatty
Alfred Ollivant
Alice Duer Miller
Alice Turner Curtis
Alice Dunbar
Allen Chapman
Ambrose Bierce
Amelia E. Barr
Amory H. Bradford
Andrew Lang
Andrew McFarland Davis
Andy Adams
Anna Alice Chapin
Anna Sewell
Annie Besant
Annie Hamilton Donnell
Annie Payson Call
Annie Roe Carr
Annonaymous
Anton Chekhov
Arnold Bennett
Arthur Conan Doyle
Arthur M. Winfield
Arthur Ransome
Arthur Schnitzler
Atticus
B.H. Baden-Powell
B. M. Bower
B. C. Chatterjee
Baroness Emmuska Orczy
Baroness Orczy
Basil King
Bayard Taylor
Ben Macomber
Bertha Muzzy Bower
Bjornstjerne Bjornson
Booth Tarkington
Boyd Cable
Bram Stoker
C. Collodi
C. E. Orr

C. M. Ingleby
Carolyn Wells
Catherine Parr Traill
Charles A. Eastman
Charles Amory Beach
Charles Dickens
Charles Dudley Warner
Charles Farrar Browne
Charles Ives
Charles Kingsley
Charles Klein
Charles Hanson Towne
Charles Lathrop Pack
Charles Romyn Dake
Charles Whibley
Charles Willing Beale
Charlotte M. Braeme
Charlotte M. Yonge
Charlotte Perkins Stetson
Clair W. Hayes
Clarence Day Jr.
Clarence E. Mulford
Clemence Housman
Confucius
Coningsby Dawson
Cornelis DeWitt Wilcox
Cyril Burleigh
D. H. Lawrence
Daniel Defoe
David Garnett
Dinah Craik
Don Carlos Janes
Donald Keyhoe
Dorothy Kilner
Dougan Clark
Douglas Fairbanks
E. Nesbit
E.P.Roe
E. Phillips Oppenheim
Earl Barnes
Edgar Rice Burroughs
Edith Van Dyne
Edith Wharton
Edward Everett Hale
Edward J. O'Biren
Edward S. Ellis
Edwin L. Arnold
Eleanor Atkins
Eliot Gregory

Elizabeth Gaskell
Elizabeth McCracken
Elizabeth Von Arnim
Ellem Key
Emerson Hough
Emilie F. Carlen
Emily Dickinson
Enid Bagnold
Enilor Macartney Lane
Erasmus W. Jones
Ernie Howard Pie
Ethel May Dell
Ethel Turner
Ethel Watts Mumford
Eugenie Foa
Eugene Wood
Eustace Hale Ball
Evelyn Everett-green
Everard Cotes
F. H. Cheley
F. J. Cross
F. Marion Crawford
Federick Austin Ogg
Ferdinand Ossendowski
Francis Bacon
Francis Darwin
Frances Hodgson Burnett
Frances Parkinson Keyes
Frank Gee Patchin
Frank Harris
Frank Jewett Mather
Frank L. Packard
Frank V. Webster
Frederic Stewart Isham
Frederick Trevor Hill
Frederick Winslow Taylor
Friedrich Kerst
Friedrich Nietzsche
Fyodor Dostoyevsky
G.A. Henty
G.K. Chesterton
Gabrielle E. Jackson
Garrett P. Serviss
Gaston Leroux
George A. Warren
George Ade
Geroge Bernard Shaw
George Durston
George Ebers

George Eliot
George Gissing
George MacDonald
George Meredith
George Orwell
George Sylvester Viereck
George Tucker
George W. Cable
George Wharton James
Gertrude Atherton
Gordon Casserly
Grace E. King
Grace Gallatin
Grace Greenwood
Grant Allen
Guillermo A. Sherwell
Gulielma Zollinger
Gustav Flaubert
H. A. Cody
H. B. Irving
H.C. Bailey
H. G. Wells
H. H. Munro
H. Irving Hancock
H. Rider Haggard
H. W. C. Davis
Haldeman Julius
Hall Caine
Hamilton Wright Mabie
Hans Christian Andersen
Harold Avery
Harold McGrath
Harriet Beecher Stowe
Harry Castlemon
Harry Coghill
Harry Houidini
Hayden Carruth
Helent Hunt Jackson
Helen Nicolay
Hendrik Conscience
Hendy David Thoreau
Henri Barbusse
Henrik Ibsen
Henry Adams
Henry Ford
Henry Frost
Henry James
Henry Jones Ford
Henry Seton Merriman
Henry W Longfellow
Herbert A. Giles

Herbert Carter
Herbert N. Casson
Herman Hesse
Hildegard G. Frey
Homer
Honore De Balzac
Horace B. Day
Horace Walpole
Horatio Alger Jr.
Howard Pyle
Howard R. Garis
Hugh Lofting
Hugh Walpole
Humphry Ward
Ian Maclaren
Inez Haynes Gillmore
Irving Bacheller
Isabel Hornibrook
Israel Abrahams
Ivan Turgenev
J.G.Austin
J. Henri Fabre
J. M. Barrie
J. Macdonald Oxley
J. S. Fletcher
J. S. Knowles
J. Storer Clouston
Jack London
Jacob Abbott
James Allen
James Andrews
James Baldwin
James Branch Cabell
James DeMille
James Joyce
James Lane Allen
James Lane Allen
James Oliver Curwood
James Oppenheim
James Otis
James R. Driscoll
Jane Austen
Jane L. Stewart
Janet Aldridge
Jens Peter Jacobsen
Jerome K. Jerome
John Burroughs
John Cournos
John F. Kennedy
John Gay
John Glasworthy

John Habberton
John Joy Bell
John Kendrick Bangs
John Milton
John Philip Sousa
Jonas Lauritz Idemil Lie
Jonathan Swift
Joseph A. Altsheler
Joseph Carey
Joseph Conrad
Joseph E. Badger Jr
Joseph Hergesheimer
Joseph Jacobs
Jules Vernes
Julian Hawthrone
Julie A Lippmann
Justin Huntly McCarthy
Kakuzo Okakura
Kenneth Grahame
Kenneth McGaffey
Kate Langley Bosher
Kate Langley Bosher
Katherine Cecil Thurston
Katherine Stokes
L. A. Abbot
L. T. Meade
L. Frank Baum
Latta Griswold
Laura Dent Crane
Laura Lee Hope
Laurence Housman
Lawrence Beasley
Leo Tolstoy
Leonid Andreyev
Lewis Carroll
Lewis Sperry Chafer
Lilian Bell
Lloyd Osbourne
Louis Hughes
Louis Tracy
Louisa May Alcott
Lucy Fitch Perkins
Lucy Maud Montgomery
Luther Benson
Lydia Miller Middleton
Lyndon Orr
M. Corvus
M. H. Adams
Margaret E. Sangster
Margret Howth
Margaret Vandercook

Margret Penrose
Maria Edgeworth
Maria Thompson Daviess
Mariano Azuela
Marion Polk Angellotti
Mark Overton
Mark Twain
Mary Austin
Mary Catherine Crowley
Mary Cole
Mary Hastings Bradley
Mary Roberts Rinehart
Mary Rowlandson
M. Wollstonecraft Shelley
Maud Lindsay
Max Beerbohm
Myra Kelly
Nathaniel Hawthrone
Nicolo Machiavelli
O. F. Walton
Oscar Wilde
Owen Johnson
P.G. Wodehouse
Paul and Mabel Thorne
Paul G. Tomlinson
Paul Severing
Percy Brebner
Peter B. Kyne
Plato
R. Derby Holmes
R. L. Stevenson
R. S. Ball
Rabindranath Tagore
Rahul Alvares
Ralph Bonehill
Ralph Henry Barbour
Ralph Victor
Ralph Waldo Emmerson
Rene Descartes
Rex Beach

Rex E. Beach
Richard Harding Davis
Richard Jefferies
Richard Le Gallienne
Robert Barr
Robert Frost
Robert Gordon Anderson
Robert L. Drake
Robert Lansing
Robert Lynd
Robert Michael Ballantyne
Robert W. Chambers
Rosa Nouchette Carey
Rudyard Kipling
Samuel B. Allison
Samuel Hopkins Adams
Sarah Bernhardt
Sarah C. Hallowell
Selma Lagerlof
Sherwood Anderson
Sigmund Freud
Standish O'Grady
Stanley Weyman
Stella Benson
Stella M. Francis
Stephen Crane
Stewart Edward White
Stijn Streuvels
Swami Abhedananda
Swami Parmananda
T. S. Ackland
T. S. Arthur
The Princess Der Ling
Thomas A. Janvier
Thomas A Kempis
Thomas Anderton
Thomas Bailey Aldrich
Thomas Bulfinch
Thomas De Quincey
Thomas Dixon

Thomas H. Huxley
Thomas Hardy
Thomas More
Thornton W. Burgess
U. S. Grant
Valentine Williams
Various Authors
Vaughan Kester
Victor Appleton
Victoria Cross
Virginia Woolf
Wadsworth Camp
Walter Camp
Walter Scott
Washington Irving
Wilbur Lawton
Wilkie Collins
Willa Cather
Willard F. Baker
William Dean Howells
William le Queux
W. Makepeace Thackeray
William W. Walter
William Shakespeare
Winston Churchill
Yei Theodora Ozaki
Yogi Ramacharaka
Young E. Allison
Zane Grey

www.ingramcontent.com/pod-product-compliance
Lightning Source LLC
Chambersburg PA
CBHW020503100426
42813CB00030B/3090/J